DRAWING ARCHITECTURE

DRAWING ARCHITECTURE

A Creative Approach
By Paul Hogarth

Preface by Sir Hugh Casson

WATSON-GUPTILL PUBLICATIONS / NEW YORK
PITMAN PUBLISHING / LONDON

First published 1973 in the United States and Canada by Watson-Guptill Publications,
a division of Billboard Publications, Inc.,
165 West 46 Street, New York, N.Y.

Published simultaneously in Great Britain by Sir Isaac Pitman & Sons Ltd.,
39 Parker Street, Kingsway, London WC2B 5PB
U.K. ISBN 0–273–00181–7

Manufactured in Japan

Library of Congress Cataloging in Publication Data
Hogarth, Paul, 1917–
    Drawing architecture.

    1. Architectural drawing.   I. Title.
NA2700.H72   720'.28   72–8820
ISBN 0–8230–1363–4

First Printing, 1973

Acknowledgments

Fine buildings are a precious heritage and I support all those who wish to preserve them. However, it is imagination, not conservation, that is the determining factor in learning to draw architecture with any degree of skill. Creative drawings can be made of the ugliest buildings, providing you know how.

This book grew out of a desire to communicate my experiences with drawing architecture during my professional career. Again, Watson-Guptill's indefatigable editorial director, Donald Holden, rose to the occasion and encouraged me to write it. I also think that I was encouraged by the success of my earlier books in this series; they made me feel that there was room for an adult approach to the "how-to" book. So, while expressing my special thanks to Don Holden for his continuing confidence in my writing, I should also like to extend my thanks to include you, the reader.

I should like to thank the following publishers, museums, libraries, and editors without whose courteous cooperation many of the illustrations could not have been included: the editors of *Horizon* magazine, New York; the editors of *Lithopinion,* and Local One, Amalgamated Lithographers of America, New York; the editors of *Boys' Life* magazine, New York; Cassell and Company, London; Doubleday & Company, Inc., New York; the editors of the *Daily Telegraph Magazine,* London; Bernard Geis Associates, New York; Hill & Wang, Inc., New York; the Hutchinson Publishing Group, London; Lawrence & Wishart, London; Library of Congress, Washington, D.C.; *Panorama* magazine, Milan; the *Philadelphia Inquirer,* Philadelphia; *Playboy* magazine, Chicago; Penguin Books, London; the editors of *Fortune, Sports Illustrated, Life, New York Times Magazine* and Time-Life Books, New York; the Riveredge Foundation, Calgary, Alberta, Canada; *Smithsonian* magazine, the Smithsonian Institution, Washington, D.C.; the Shelbourne Hotel, Dublin; Studio Vista Ltd., London; the Strathmore Paper Company, West Springfield, Massachusetts; Smith, Kline and French Laboratories, Philadelphia; and Wydownictwo Artystczno-Graficzne, Warsaw. All of these have generously allowed drawings of mine (which they either own or have the publication rights to) to be included in this book.

For friendly assistance in the loan of originals, proofs, photographs, and transparencies, I should like to personally express my appreciation to the following: John Anstey, editor of the *Daily Telegraph Magazine,* London; Walter Allner, art director, *Fortune;* Richard Gangel, art director, *Sports Illustrated;* Robert Hallock, art director, *Lithopinion;* Diana Klemin, art director, Doubleday & Company; Andrew Lessin, art director, *Boys' Life* magazine; Arthur Paul, art director, *Playboy;* Bill Roseman, Vice-President of the Lambert Agency, New York; and last, but certainly not least, Edward Riley, my art agent in New York; and Sir Hugh Casson, wise colleague and friendly spirit throughout the years.

Finally, I would also like to gratefully acknowledge permission of the owners to reproduce copyrighted works not in my possession or works not in the possession of a publisher or of a magazine.

Paul Hogarth
Deya, Majorca

Preface

Architecture has always attracted the artist. In every century and every country he can be found happily drawing palaces, cottages, churches, farmsteads, or just doodling with a set of columns, steps, and urns to round off—with dignified geometry—his portrait or his landscape. The artist has always known that, nice as it may be to look at a place, there's no better way of knowing (and remembering) what it is really like than by drawing it. Not that buildings—which are as varied, lovable, and unexpected as faces—are any easier to draw than people. But at least they stand still—and don't complain afterwards! Nor should they, if they are lucky enough to have been recorded by so skilled, experienced, and affectionate a draughtsman as the author of this book.

On the pages that follow Paul Hogarth passes on to us some of the wisdom—sharpened by his world travels—that he has acquired, and illustrates it with drawings that positively crackle with wit and athletic observation. He deals with the practical problems of tools and equipment, viewpoints, composition, and perspective. He suggests methods of dealing with certain architectural periods or building types: castles—"attack them like a soldier"; the Grand Manner—"start with country houses"; and Victoriana—"don't be frightened; it's lovely once you're into it." He advises preliminary reading and research, studying architectural details (door handles, railings, and cornices) in advance, stalking your subject from many angles before moving in to strike, and copious, alert note-taking. His advice on everything is imaginative, sensible, and freshly phrased. Finally, like every good artist, he knows that architecture is more than buildings, however grand, famous, or intricate they may be. It is also the small things that matter: paving stones and litter bins; lettering and manhole covers; beggars and policemen; and pillar boxes and shoes. All these things together with light, texture, smells, and movement make one place different from another. Only by noting and then drawing all these architectural variables will the artist recognize, love, and fully understand architecture.

Sir Hugh Casson
Professor of Interior Design
Royal College of Art, London

Contents

Introduction

As the dictionaries define it, architecture is the art, the science, or the style of building. For me, architecture is something *very* different. More often than not it is the embodiment of a daydream about a palace or pub occupied by the memories of people and events long since gone. Drawing architecture can also involve a preoccupation with the filth and clamor of industry. At other times, it is more of an esthetic appreciation of the graceful strength of a cathedral or skyscraper, or the coiled and sinuously rich stonework of a Victorian apartment house, or even the complex interplay in the hand-hewn beams of a medieval manor. Therefore, drawing architecture is my way of expressing a personal obsession with both the past and the present; it is my reaction to the unseen—all that which exists within the context of a visually acceptable shape, or structure, that has been molded by the ideas and ambitions of its time.

Because I think of architecture in this way—not as a dry exercise in perspective or an exact rendering of geometrical elements—drawing buildings of any period (classical or commercial vernacular) becomes a matter of personal interpretation. And so I have always regarded it as one of the most adventurous and spirited areas of my work.

At the beginning, I did not see architecture in these terms. As an art student my head was filled with the problem of perspective rather than the chronicles of history. After spending many hours poring over an arrangement, establishing vanishing points, and fixing horizon lines in relation to the picture plane, etc., buildings ceased to have any significance for me. They were merely the object of a complex geometrical exercise which I sought every opportunity to avoid. Again, as in life drawing, it was the musty, frustrating conventions of unenlightened academic instruction which conspired to thwart and even destroy my enthusiasm.

What saved the situation was a series of occasional slide lectures, euphemistically entitled "History of Style." In these lectures we were told about the elements of architectural decoration and motifs (geometrical lines, natural foliage, animals, and figures); the Greek and Roman orders of architecture; the great Gothic cathedrals of the Middle Ages; Victorian follies; mechanical marvels; and American skyscrapers.

The lectures were largely based on Sir Banister Fletcher's definitive book, *A History of Architecture* (14th edition, London, 1948) and Franz Sales Meyer's *Handbook of Ornament* (now available as a Dover paperback). It was heavy going, but the lecturer, whose name I've forgotten, did sometimes add a personal view which enlivened the formidable mass of verbal and pictorial data.

My interest in architecture, therefore, preceded any idea of how I would actually *draw* a building. There was no one around who might have ended my dilemma by saying "why don't you think of them as monsters or even odd-shaped people?" Such a suggestion would have enabled me to see buildings as *entities* and *shapes,* and not as vast, anonymous piles of masonry that had to be faithfully rendered with an HB graphite pencil. I also had to evolve my own subject selection. It took a great deal of time, wandering, and self-study before I could draw architecture the way I wanted.

After a series of false starts, I began to move towards a breakthrough. During 1953–54, I went on a series of travels in war-shattered Europe and Asia. Historical architecture began to qualify as a subject for my pencil, and I sat before the fine old palaces and cathedrals of Czechoslovakia, Germany, Poland, and Italy mourning their loss or celebrating their reconstruction. In China, I witnessed the dramatic building of large-scale industrial architecture which was to proclaim an immense social revolution.

Of course, more often than not, I failed in my attempts, but one satisfaction kept me at it; the more I tackled the buildings that aroused my sense of history, the more confidence I acquired. I discovered, too, that after I began my explorations into the potentials of different media, I found that very often a repertoire of pencils, inks, markers, and watercolor might well be the key to depicting more complex subjects. My drawing became more essentially architectural; the emphasis on either line, structure, or monumentality produced a generally expressive effect of rhythmic order laced with occasional fantasy.

The capacity to draw architecture is, therefore, really a form of understanding the social and cultural aspects of history. Once you have a questioning curiosity inside you, you need only discover a way to express it pictorially. My previous books, *Creative Pencil Drawing* and *Creative Ink Drawing* will help you in this respect because they focus on various means of expression. While specific techniques are summarized where they arise, *Drawing Architecture* concentrates primarily on the problems involved in interpreting the style of architecture that is so interwoven with the fabric of history. Sometimes the power of a drawing is found not so much in its faithfulness to the subject but in its revelation of something *you did not know or understand before.* I hope you will find, as I have, that drawing architecture can give you a nostalgia for the past, as well as a greater awareness of the present.

1
Tools and Materials

Drawing architecture requires both intelligent and creative use of tools and materials. These include graphite pencils or charcoal leads, which are suitable for working in sketchbooks on location and for drawing on sheets of paper in the relative privacy of the studio. Also needed are inks, colored markers, and watercolors which are suitable for drawing on papers and boards. What medium to use and what equipment to carry can be resolved by considering how much time you have and where you will be working, as well as whether your drawing or painting is for yourself, for an individual client, or for publication.

An awareness of tools and materials, plus a lively appreciation of their esthetic relationship to each other, is vital to your continued development as an artist. Whenever and whatever you draw, try to acquire the habit of using the right kind of pencil, pen, brush, or marker for the appropriate paper. Familiarize yourself with their potentials and idiosyncrasies. Stay with the tools and materials you feel at home with until you get bored. Only then will it be time to get acquainted with new tools and materials.

BEGIN SIMPLY

Graphic media today cover such a wide range, including both traditional and modern tools and materials, that choice may be difficult. Hardly a year goes by without the appearance of some new fountain pen or improved type of felt-tip or fiber-tip pen or marker, or new, brilliantly transparent pigments and colored inks. It becomes difficult to resist buying them and trying them all out. While this is a good thing to do, I would advise holding off until you have gained practice with the more basic black-and-white tools.

Drawing architecture is a way of expressing a personal reaction to style or history. To draw

House in Alaverdova Square, Tbilisi, Georgia, U.S.S.R., 1967. *(Right) I combined pencil with watercolor to make this study of the poet Lermontov's house in the old Kura district. I drew in the onlookers with a Faber 702 sketching pencil. From* A Russian Journey: from Suzdal to Samarkand, *1969. Courtesy Cassell and Company, London; and Hill & Wang, Inc., New York. Reproduced by permission of the owner, Pat Douthwaite, Deya, Majorca.*

TBILISI Lermontov
House, Alaverdova
Square in the Kura
district

architecture, even imaginatively, you must be able to define shape or structure in a lively, fluent way. Start with a 3B graphite pencil and a sketchbook before you move on to ink, watercolor, markers, and mixed media.

PENCILS

The choice of a pencil depends a great deal on your approach and even your state of mind when you confront the subject. There are days when I can only draw with a strong heavy line; other days it may be a restrained or delicate one. If you share my uncertain temperament, then be sure to carry, as I do, a whole batch of graphite pencils, differing widely in softness and size. A wide choice of pencils enables me to achieve the maximum variety of line, which is particularly desirable if certain details require emphasis or careful delineation.

For example, with a 2B or 3B pencil, I can define the complexities of a medieval archway or chimney stack much more precisely than with, say, a 6B which I might use for a rainpipe or window to achieve a degree of contrast. In the standard sizes, reliable brands like American Venus, Hardtmuth Koh-i-noor, or Eagle Turquoise are recommended. Since I work a great deal with graphite pencils, I also carry a batch of pencil lengtheners (nickel-plated holders with sliding rings).

I also use much softer, black graphite pencils with which I can develop a drawing by heavily accenting shapes or areas. The American Veriblack (in Britain, the Royal Sovereign Black Prince) I find excellent. But my favorite continues to be the German Faber 702, a lustrously soft graphite pencil that performs well on almost any kind of paper—good, bad, or indifferent. But you do need to keep it sharpened with a good, sharp knife. So carry a Stanley 5900 or an X-Acto No. 2 medium-sized handle knife with you, and do not forget a spare packet of No. 22 blades, because the 702 pencil dulls them quickly.

You may also find Conté charcoal leads and Hardtmuth charcoal crayons well suited to drawing architecture. Both work best on the kind of paper expressly made for them.

Conté *Pierre Noir* leads are particularly suitable for vigorous drawings where a minimum amount of detail is required. Hardtmuth cray-

ons, on the other hand, are much more suitable for broader, looser drawings which strive only for mood or atmosphere; the crayons are graded medium, soft, and extra soft. However, leads and crayons are difficult to use without covering your paper with black fingermarks. It is advisable, therefore, to use them in a holder, preferably the hexagonal or milled type which permits a firm grip.

Charcoal pencils possess the same virtues as charcoal leads and are, perhaps, less inhibiting if you prefer the familiar feel of a pencil to that of an instrument. They are particularly suitable for drawing chunky or globular buildings in a broad, bold style. Conté and Hardtmuth without a doubt make the best, but Eagle's Charco pencils—available in four degrees: 6B (extra soft), 4B (soft), 2B (medium soft), and HB (firm)—are also recommended.

If you use soft graphite charcoal leads and pencils, you will have to fix them to avoid smudging; the sooner you can do this, the better. Use fixative in a spray can; it is both convenient and efficient. I use Blair, Eagle, or Krylon workable matte fixative; all three provide a compatible working surface if reworking becomes necessary.

PENS

My choice of a pen is usually confined to tough, resilient school nibs; the Spencerian No. 5 is a good one. It gives me a strong basic line. If I need something extra, or more than one thickness, or a more spidery line, I indulge in a fine, flexible artist's nib like a Gillot 290 or 303, or an Esterbrook 355 or 357. I make sure to fit them in a good holder. A spindly penholder—for example, the so-called mapping pen—usually cramps the fingers; when this happens, a line can completely lose vitality. Be sure to get a penholder that feels much the same in your hand as your own fountain pen or ballpoint.

For continuous drawing where I need to work fast without interruption, a fountain pen is essential. Strangely enough, in my experience anyway, the tough and yet inexpensive Esterbrook pen and the Osmiroid sketchpen, stand up best of all to the vigorous pressures of my drawing. I have also used Parker and Sheaffer fountain pens, which, of course, I highly recommend. Try out the pen's nib before you buy it.

Udarnik Movie Theatre, Moscow, 1967. *Modern architecture can be depicted with the simplest tools and materials. Because I had very little time to spend on this drawing, I decided to use just a brush and a pencil. I drew it in a 15″ x 20″ sketchbook of English Glastonbury Antique paper using a pointed Japanese brush with Higgins Eternal ink and a Faber 702 sketching pencil. From A Russian Journey: from Suzdal to Samarkand, 1969. Courtesy Cassell and Company, London; and Hill & Wang, Inc., New York.*

St. Mary Panachrantos, Istanbul, Turkey, 1966. *This is one of a series of historical illustrations depicting life in twelfth-century Constantinople that I made for Time-Life Books. The Church of St. Mary Panachrantos is intact and in remarkably good shape despite its great age. Byzantine architects lavished a great deal of attention on interior spaces and mosaics. Outside decorations were left to imaginative masons who spaced out stone with friezes and rosettes of brick imbedded in colored mortar. To convey something of these textural effects, I first blocked out the shape of the church with a large Japanese brush charged with washes of diluted Pelikan permanent black writing ink. Then, I painted the decorative masonry with Winsor & Newton No. 4 and No. 6 sable brushes in undiluted Higgins India ink. I used Daler drawing paper as a surface and a Gillot 303 nib to delineate the barred windows. From Byzantium, a volume in "The Great Ages of Man" series, Time-Life Books. © 1966, Time, Inc., New York.*

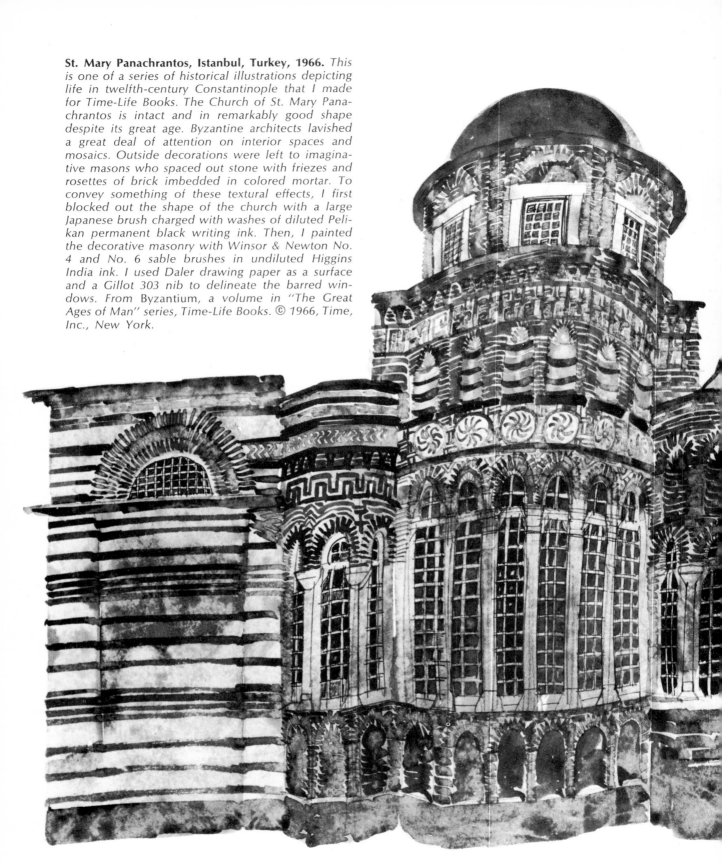

This is the part which most often determines and influences the way you will draw.

Ballpoints and fiber-tip pens—as useful as they undoubtedly are for drawing rapidly and continuously in a small sketchbook, or making notes for additions to larger drawings—are not really tools that can be used to advantage in drawing architecture. A good ballpoint, fiber-tip pen is worth the extra cost for the more fluid and expressive line it produces, but I do not find much use for one when I am out drawing a building, other than to make notes for a composition, or some detail I may have overlooked.

BRUSHES

Many of my drawings of architecture tend to be a combination of drawing and painting. Therefore, the choice of good brushes is extremely important. Generally, I use two kinds: Chinese brushes and watercolor brushes. For black-and-white work, I use medium and large, pointed Japanese or Chinese brushes which are made from the tail hair of a wide variety of animals. The finest quality are comparatively inexpensive and stand up to a remarkable amount of punishment with every kind of drawing ink. Moreover, if I use them to draw with, I can get a fine line by using the point and a thicker one by increasing the downward pressure on the brush.

When working with color, however, I use watercolor brushes like Winsor & Newton's artist's quality red sables, available in sizes from 00 to 14. I use mostly Nos. 0, 6, and 10. Watercolor brushes are also made of squirrel hair, sometimes called camel hair. But these are soft and will not spring back, and a brush that has no spring does not perform as a brush should. You can test for spring by wetting a brush to a point and dragging it lightly over your thumbnail. It should not droop but should spring back If I have to economize when buying brushes (they can be expensive), my big wash brush can be squirrel hair.

CLEANING AND STORING BRUSHES

No matter what brushes you choose or prefer to work with, not only will they last longer, but they will work more efficiently if you take care of them. Never forget to wash them out thoroughly in warm soapy water as soon as con-

Washington Arch, Washington Square, New York, 1962. *Ink is able to delineate architecture of every kind with commendable precision and accuracy. I used a Spencerian nib for Washington Arch and the apartment block rising behind it. I used a Gillot 303 nib for the more flexible relaxed drawing of the trees and the figures. The drawing was done on Saunders writing paper. From Brendan Behan's New York, 1964. Courtesy Hutchinson Publishing Group, London; and Bernard Geis Associates, New York.*

venient. Brushes should be carried, or stored, *not* in your paintbox but in an air-tight separate container or brushcase. In this way, they can be more easily protected against their two great enemies, moths and mildew. The clothes moth attacks the point of the brush; mildew attacks the brush at the root of the ferrule. Put your brushes away absolutely dry with a camphor or naphthalene ball.

INKS

Drawing inks for artists are sold in two varieties: *waterproof,* which (after it has completely dried) will stand up to washes of watercolor, marker strokes, or diluted washes of the same ink; and *soluble,* which may be washed away with water, a clean brush, and blotting paper. Both waterproof and soluble inks may be freely diluted with water. The best waterproof inks are the India inks made by Higgins (4415 Black Label), Reeves, Winsor & Newton, and Pelikan. Grumbacher's black India (which also adheres to acetate vinyl without "crawling") contains lixium, a useful solvent that cleans your pen. However, such inks should not be used in a fountain pen because they invariably clog the nib. Fountain pens work better with soluble inks; the best are made by Mont Blanc, Sheaffer (Skrip), and Higgins (4425 Red Label), though a convenient compromise is Pelican's Fount India —a fairly waterproof ink designed for use in fountain pens.

The heavier waterproof inks are useful whenever I want to use a wash or watercolor over them, and I do not want the original ink drawing to lose strength or incisiveness. On the other hand, soluble inks sometimes have the advantage because they can be reduced in tone if I decide the rest of the drawing needs greater emphasis. My procedure is to continually apply washes of clean and, if possible, warm water with a large brush, firmly blotting each application before cleaning the brush and applying the next wash. If I use colored inks, I am careful to choose those which mix freely with each other and with black and white.

MARKERS

Whenever I need to depict an elaborate building, I may use color to help emphasize any unusual point of interest. My choice is usually a combination of color markers and watercolors. Let me discuss markers first. Provided they are of high quality they can be adapted to almost every kind of drawing. Moreover, they save a prodigious amount of effort whenever I am short on time. Because I always seem to be working against the clock, markers have frequently provided an exhilarating series of shortcuts to add instant-drying color to big drawings which would otherwise not have been possible to complete on the spot, or even in my hotel room.

Markers come in two main types: fiber-tip markers and felt-tip ones; each are available with different points. Fiber-tip markers usually have fine points and are, therefore, ideal for making incisive, detailed drawings. Here are the best I have found: the Japanese Pentel Sign Pens, available in eight colors and in small and large sizes; the German Faber-Castell Presto, also available in three basic colors; and the Esterbrook Color Pen which comes in eight colors.

For finer, more detailed drawing there is the Fine Point Studio watercolor liner made by Eberhard Faber. This remarkable instrument is available in three different sets of colors— twelve basic, twelve complementary, and twelve combination groups. Set 873 contains all thirty-six colors, fitted into a rotating carousel table.

Avoid the cheap markers that are made primarily for office or dispatching purposes. Not only are the colors crude, but the inks (really a dye) will penetrate almost any kind of paper. Although more expensive, felt-tip Studio Magic Markers and Faber Design Markettes are actually more economical because they last longer, do not stain your paper, and are, therefore, much easier to control.

Magic Markers and Design Markettes are available in an ever-increasing range of colors. They differ in appearance; the Magic Markers come in small, bottle-like containers and have a wide chisel tip. I myself prefer to use the Markettes which, because of their elongated pen-like shape, can be held like a thick pen or pencil. They are available with a wide chisel tip in seventy-two colors, or with a pointed tip in twenty-four. Cooper Color, Inc., makes an AD marker that has 40% more ink than others and comes in 102 colors with a choice of points: wedge, bullet, blunt, fine line, and brush.

WATERCOLORS

I may not always have the time to work with watercolors all the way through; nevertheless, I find them essential for developing—in the calm of my hotel room or my studio—work that I was unable to finish on location. Even on location, I use a wash or two of translucent watercolor to augment the markers.

The watercolors need not be the more expensive artist's quality either. But if I do buy regular quality watercolors, I make sure they are made by a reputable firm like Winsor & Newton or Grumbacher. I have found their scholastic colors excellent. However, if I do have an exhibit in the back of my mind which will mean prolonged or constant exposure to light, I will use artist's quality to guarantee that they do not fade; although certain colors, however finely made, will always fade.

Winsor & Newton's artist's watercolors are the very best that money can buy and have a brilliance and freshness which is sustained on almost any kind of paper. Moreover, they print SL (selected list) on the labels of their permanent colors. I avoid the elaborate expensive watercolor sets or outfits and buy my colors separately, carrying them in a standard 4½″ × 9½″ aluminum, double palette box which has baked enamel mixing wells under a lift-out tray in the lid; the tray holds fifteen tubes. I usually buy small tubes of artist's watercolors so that very little can be wasted by drying up through excessive heat or infrequent use. Sometimes on a long trip I also carry a box of extra tubes. If I am using regular quality watercolors, I buy the 3″ size.

The only set I do carry is a space-saving 4″ × 6½″ sixteen-pan aluminum box of German Marabu watercolors. These inexpensive colors cannot be compared with Winsor & Newton's artist's colors but they are very brilliant; they leave no stains, no edges, can be washed off, and are generally lightproof. They also come in round 1″ pans.

SUGGESTED PALETTE

A list of colors is, of course, a personal choice but I find the following most useful—although I generally work with fewer colors, mixing them if and when required.

ultramarine blue	sepia or Van Dyke brown
Prussian blue	raw umber
cobalt blue	burnt sienna
emerald green	Venetian red
viridian	vermilion
lemon yellow	light red
yellow ochre	alizarin crimson

A small tube of Chinese white and large ones of lamp or ivory black and Paynes Gray complete my box.

PAPERS

Ink, pencil, and watercolor (in fact, all drawing media) work best on the papers originally designed for them. The only exceptions to this general rule are the soft graphite pencils like the Faber 702 or the Veriblack 315. They seem to work just as well on Bristol board, layout paper, or tracing paper as they do on good quality papers especially made for drawing. Nevertheless, these media—ink, pencil, and watercolor—are at their best on drawing papers (called "cartridge" in Great Britain) such as American Strathmore, English Hollingworth Kent Mill or French Canson.

Because of the greater amount of detail and the possible extra use of color, I find good quality drawing paper is both vital and essential. Paper of good quality can be readily identified by its pure white color and closely-grained texture. On such paper almost any HB graphite pencil or pen will leave a lively expressive line. On an off-white, coarser-grained drawing paper of poor quality, pencils and pens leave a tired unexpressive line. They behave unpredictably; they may sometimes be effective but usually are not.

Charcoal pencils or Conté leads also work well on versatile Strathmore, Hollingworth Kent Mill, or Canson papers; but they, too, are most at home on the papers made for them: the textured, so-called laid papers, with their finely ribbed surface or parallel lines, like Strathmore Charcoal and French or Italian Ingres papers. Strathmore and Ingres papers are made in colors and can be obtained both in single sheets and sketchbook form.

Inks of every kind work well on Strathmore, Hollingworth Kent Mill, and Canson drawing papers. But ink is more at home—at least with a pen if not a brush—on the paper devised for the pen nib—the super smooth-surfaced Bristol board.

However, felt-tip markers and fiber-tip pens pose a different problem. Even though they have been perfected, their indiscriminate use is dangerous because they may unexpectedly bleed or stain on poor or even medium quality papers. The only way to avoid this spreading effect is to use high quality drawing paper or Bristol board.

By itself, watercolor—or mixed media involving watercolor, markers, graphite pencils, and ink—requires paper of a good and reliable quality. With mixed media, each medium must work satisfactorily with the other. On paper of poor quality, watercolor is seldom effective over areas or shapes filled or drawn with markers. Moreover, watercolor dries unevenly on the weaker fibers of poor quality papers. The result is that pencil or pen work is in danger of being dishearteningly unsatisfactory. Indeed, the weakened fibers, even when dry, seldom stand up to such a strain. Here, once again, the multipurpose Strathmore, Hollingworth, and Canson drawing papers fulfill the demands of mixed media work as does Strathmore Bristol board.

SKETCHBOOKS

When drawing architecture on location, I work in sketchbooks simply because they can be carried easily in hand, pocket, or bag. The size I use will vary according to subject and location, but generally the most common sizes are 11" × 14" or 15" × 20". I will sometimes work over two facing pages of a sketchbook, because I usually think in terms of a drawing as a shape occupying either one page or two. If two, I will work on an area 20" deep by 30" wide. It is not possible to obtain this size or proportion in the average stock-size sketchbook. They would not open like a book anyway but like a shorthand pad. Moreover, I would have to work on the wrong and right sides of the paper.

The Toly-Telpakthuryon Caravanserai, Bukhara, U.S.S.R., 1967. *A soft graphite sketching pencil is an ideal medium for drawing the free-form shapes of early oriental architecture. This "Gaudí-esque" caravanserai, or inn, (where carpet salesmen were put up) dates from the time when Bukhara was the most important center of the hand-woven carpet trade. I made this drawing in a 15" x 20" sketchbook of Glastonbury Antique drawing paper with a Faber 702 sketching pencil. With a Japanese brush I painted in the wash of Higgins India ink and blotted it. An unpublished drawing from my trip to the U.S.S.R. in 1967.*

Plaza San Jaime, Manacor, Majorca, 1963. *Perhaps this unusual stone fountain celebrates a prize catch of fish. At any rate, it made a good focal point for my interpretation of a quiet Majorcan fishing port. I drew it entirely with 3B and 7B Venus graphite pencils on Saunders paper. From Majorca Observed, 1965. Courtesy Cassell and Company, London; and Doubleday & Company, Inc., New York.*

So I buy a quantity of good quality drawing paper (a recent favorite has been the superb English Glastonbury Antique) and have a sketchbook made which will give me thirty double-page sheets. Although folded, they can be pressed flat after being easily detached when it is filled. But if you do not have access to a co-operative bookbinder in an art school, technical college, library, or small printing establishment, a spiral-bound sketchbook of Strathmore or Canson drawing paper can be worked on both sides. If required, the two separate pages can be trimmed and flat mounted together later. But the pages have to be truly joined; so take them to an art or photography supplies store where they can be dry (electrically) mounted on thin, medium, or thick board. I also carry a small sketchbook (A5 size, 5⅞″ × 8¼″) of drawing or cartridge paper in which I scribble notes, details, and ideas with a fountain pen, ballpoint, fiber-tip pen, marker, or pencil.

SELECTING SUITABLE EQUIPMENT

Tools and materials are two constants in an artist's life. Because of the searching and traveling in drawing architecture it is necessary to consider your selection of tools and materials carefully beforehand. Failure to do this can not only be time-consuming but demoralizing when, for example, you discover that you have left behind a particular pencil, pen, or sketchbook which might have made all the difference.

But you can vastly simplify matters by following a few basic rules. Before you pack, think of where you are going. Will you be in a large city or in a more informal place like a country village or seaside resort? How long will you stay? What will the weather be like? Are you flying, driving, or going by ship? Keep all these variables firmly in mind when selecting your materials as well as your wardrobe.

If you are taking a long trip, visiting many different areas, decide on what you will need day to day. It helps enormously to make an itinerary, because it enables you to anticipate what you may need.

Next, prepare a list of basic tools and materials: pencils, pens, brushes, ink, markers, watercolors, and papers or sketchbooks.

Once you have an idea of what you are going to take along on a sketching trip, you should consider how you are going to take it with you. If you are flying, remember the forty-four and sixty-six pound limit in tourist economy and first class respectively. Carry-on luggage must be small enough to fit under your seat (8″ × 14″ × 21″).

Although materials and equipment can be carried in a satchel or shoulder bag, I usually carry everything in a zippered leather, canvas, or plastic portfolio. I have several but the one I use most often is 4″ × 17″ × 23″ in size. This holds the bulk of my working equipment—pens, pencils, and brushes—each in light metal or plastic containers or bags; fixative in a spray can; and a plastic army canteen with fitted cup. Pencils and brushes, for example, I carry in a light, flat aluminum container 1″ × 6″ × 18″ in size. Fragile or easily damaged items, such as spare nibs, I place in aluminum boxes. Ever since disaster, in the shape of a broken ink bottle, struck a filled sketchbook, I carry ink in a plastic bottle placed in a plastic bag. Some inks (for example, Mont Blanc soluble black ink) are available in unbreakable containers. And do not forget a large box of tissues, and elastic bands—the thick and durable type. They are useful for making sure that boxes and containers do not empty out their contents inside your bag.

Finally, you should take along a portable stool. A really comfortable stool is indispensable if you draw a great deal outdoors. Drawing architecture does involve longer work periods. Keep leg cramps at bay by selecting a stool which will enable you to maintain a normal sitting posture. Preferences will vary but a good one like the French tubular artist's metal stool with leather seat and shoulder strap—or the equally good American Scott Port-A-Fold which also has a leather seat—is well worth the extra cost. For working in the country, there is the less expensive English Feathermate Seat Stick made by Buttons of Birmingham.

If you weigh under a hundred and fifty pounds (I do not), the popular aluminum folding stool with canvas seat, available in most hardware stores or Woolworth's, can be just as satisfactory—at least for the young. This completes your equipment for drawing architecture.

2
Looking at Architecture

Almost any structure that encloses space enough for people to live or work in can be called a *building*. However, the term *architecture* can only be applied to a building *designed* to have esthetic appeal, and, therefore, capable of arousing appreciation for its style and proportion, as well as its historical association. It is important to briefly discuss appreciation as a factor which will stop you dead in your tracks and move you enough to want to draw a building.

The eminent architectural historian, Nikolaus Pevsner, called such appreciation *esthetic sensation*. This, he says, may be caused by a building in three different ways. First, the esthetic sensation may be aroused by the treatment of walls, proportions of windows, the relation of wall space to window space, the relation of one story or floor to another, and ornamentation. (The delicate tracery of a fourteenth-century window, and the leaf and fruit garlands of a Wren porch are cited as examples.)

Secondly, the treatment of the exterior as a whole, its contrasts of block against block, or the effect of a pitched or flat roof or a dome may arouse this sensation. Thirdly, he concludes, there is the effect on your senses of the treatment of the interior, the sequence of rooms, the widening of a nave (of a cathedral) at the crossing, and the stately movement of a baroque staircase.

CULTIVATING ARCHITECTURAL AWARENESS

The time it may take to cultivate your faculties to receive these vibrations depends on how much effort and enthusiasm you yourself put into it. Study courses and self-study through reading outline histories such as Herbert Pothorn's *Styles of Architecture* (London, 1971 and

The Carthusian Monastery, Valldemosa, Majorca, 1963. *(Right) Memories sometimes leave a sediment of enchantment behind which colors your own attitude toward a place. Frederic Chopin and George Sand lived for several months on the isle of Majorca in 1838. It is easy to feel their presence in the rooms that they occupied in the massive-walled Cartuja, or charterhouse, of the romantically picturesque Carthusian Monastery. I drew this with various grades of Venus graphite pencils—4B, 5B, and 7B—on white Saunders paper. From Majorca Observed, 1965. Courtesy Cassell and Company, London; and Doubleday & Company, Inc., New York.*

VALLDEMOSA
Paul Hogarth

Old Houses in the Rue Royale, Vieux Carré, New Orleans, 1971. *This large watercolor drawing was made in just over two hours by using a combination of watercolors, markers, and India ink washed on an outline of soft graphite pencil. The Andrew Jackson Hotel (right) was formerly the Old Court House where General Andrew Jackson was fined a thousand dollars for contempt of court. A horse-drawn carriage with visitors came by and paused to look at the scene, so I put them in, too. I used a double sheet from my custom-made, 15" x 20" sketchbook of Glastonbury Antique paper. Reproduced by permission of the owner, Christopher Walker, Cambridge, England.*

New Orleans = Vieux Carré

HIBERNIA

Architectural Ornament, 1966–1971. *Sometimes details of buildings such as this statue that I discovered in Dublin, Ireland provide necessary atmosphere to definitely establish the style or "period" of a building.*

New York, 1972) and Pevsner's excellent *Outline of European Architecture* (Pelican paperback, London and Baltimore, 1968) can help introduce you to the general background. But, by far, the best course for a student of drawing architecture is seeing it all with your own eyes. Travel reintroduces what you may have overlooked in the context of strange and exotic surroundings. So much so, that when you return you see your environment with completely new eyes. Thus, you are more able to assess your environment graphically.

For me, an awareness of architecture began with the average introduction to it that most art students get; this was heightened by continuous travel that most art students did *not* get at the time I was in school. It took one or two trips to start me off, but after the third I felt such a remarkable degree of mounting appreciative awareness that for some time it outdistanced my capacity to depict the fine architecture I gazed at with such unrestrained enthusiasm!

As you are cultivating your awareness of architecture try not to do so like a wandering esthete, but gain your appreciation *through* the medium of your drawings—by actually drawing what you see.

APPRECIATING POPULAR ARCHITECTURE

In forthcoming chapters I intend to deal more fully with the more important or distinctive types of architecture, more or less by period. This also includes indigenous or popular styles, commonly known as vernacular architecture. But I would like to make one comment on the vernacular type beforehand, because it does constitute such an important sphere of subject matter.

Old movie theaters, suburban houses, gas stations, drug stores, bars, and even parking lots, all qualify for this category of vernacular architecture. Humble as they are beside the great edifices of the past and the gleaming skyscrapers of the present, they have provided me with some of my most exciting and enjoyable experiences. Moreover, drawing vernacular architecture often opens up new ways of seeing conventional architecture. As an old friend, the English painter Ruskin Spear, so cogently put it, "Bad architecture is a damn sight easier to draw than good!"

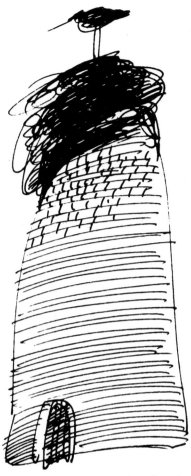

Sketchbook Study, 1966–1971. *Like the sketch on the preceding page, this architectural motif was incorporated into a larger drawing. Both these sketches were made in a pocket or small-sized sketchbook with a soft graphite pencil or, as in the case of the stork, a fountain pen.*

Practice seeking out such buildings—decade by decade if you like—and draw them with sympathy and understanding. Do not forget the clutter of signs, shingles, and billboards that invariably surrounds them.

NOSTALGIC MOTIVATION

Apart from the esthetic sensation, appreciation of achitecture springs just as readily from various associations which on the surface may appear to have little or nothing to do with architecture. In themselves, such associations frequently provide the necessary stimulus for making a more unusual interpretation. I think of my own childhood history and literature classes which played an important role in helping me develop imaginative associations of places and people.

Therefore, by virtue of what I have read, like Greek myth, I may be drawn to classical antiquity; to the mysterious anonymity of the pyramids of Egypt (recorded in the largely half-forgotten novels of Rider Haggard); and to the later revival of Greek and Roman architecture —the Renaissance—to mention just a few.

On other occasions I will remember Victor Hugo's novel *Notre Dame de Paris* when gazing on the irrational Gothic styles of the Middle Ages, with their vast buttressed cathedrals soaring above clustered teeming towns, circled by moated walls. Sometimes, I will remember the Moorish conquest of Spain which lives on in the Islamic style of architecture found there. This style spread throughout North Africa and the Middle East during the seventh century and entered Europe during the eighth century; the richly decorated palaces of Granada are good examples of this type.

Quite suddenly on location I may be confronted with a place which has played some eventful role in the life of a nation or individual. Immediately the atmosphere of that time possesses me; this historic ambiance often compels me to set down the scene on paper with even more enthusiasm than a purely esthetic appreciation of any style the building may possess would give me. Let your imagination also play its part when you draw architecture.

A Corner of Smithfield, Dublin, 1964. *One of the best ways of savoring a city is to look for a neighborhood district, preferably of the 1900's or 1920's vintage. I found this one behind the quays of the Irish capitol, complete with corner bar, pigeons, and children. I used 3B and 7B Venus graphite pencils on Saunders writing paper. Courtesy the Shelbourne Hotel, Dublin, Ireland.*

3
Selecting Your Subject

Deciding what architecture to draw is, of course, the next step. Here I may be guided by various affinities I have towards a period: for example, the Gothic eccentricities of New York apartment-house architecture in and around Gramercy Park; London movie theater "Aztec" architecture of the 1930's or Moscow's Art Nouveau style of the late 1800's. Such preferences are developed by seeing movies, or browsing through well-edited magazines, like the English *Architectural Review*. Sometimes I draw buildings typical of several different periods before discovering one which compels me to go on and make a series.

Consciously or unconsciously most of us will possess certain affinities towards one architectural idiom or lifestyle. Whatever period this may be, search for such buildings and draw them. This will sharpen your sense of selection as well as increase your awareness of style, particularly if you live in a city where observation usually becomes blunted by overfamiliarity.

RESEARCHING YOUR SUBJECT

Preliminary study of your chosen place of pilgrimage can often provide additional stimulus for making drawings. This kind of preliminary work can give you a much deeper sense of commitment if the period is unfamiliar to you.

I started completely from zero when I undertook a *Daily Telegraph Magazine* assignment to depict a Burgundian wine festival known as *Les Trois Glorieuses*—The Three Glorious Days. The story was about the testing and selling of the 1970 vintage which was bigger and better than ever before. But the architectural context was important because it served to heighten the fairy tale atmosphere of the event. Church bells chimed folksongs on the hour; there was dancing in the streets, as well as round-the-clock sampling of wines old and new in vast cellars;

Spring near the Gur Emir, Samarkand, U.S.S.R., 1967. *(Right) I combined markers and watercolor to make this seasonal impression of this historic mausoleum, the tomb of Tamurlane and other oriental monarchs. The trees, the figures, and the house were drawn in with a Faber 702 sketching pencil. From* A Russian Journey: from Suzdal to Samarkand, 1969. *Courtesy Cassell and Company, London; and Hill & Wang, Inc., New York.*

Samarkand: Spring
near the Gur Emir

Page from My Morocco Notebook, 1971. *(Above)
Before drawing buildings I usually jot down ideas
of how I might draw them. This compositional note
is for a drawing of one of the principal gates of
Fez, the Bab Guiza. I often use such notes for elaborate drawings such as the one on the opposite page.*

**Court d'Honneur, Hôtel Dieu, Hospices de Beaune,
Beaune, France, 1970.** *(Right) The fifteenth-century
Hôtel Dieu is a part of the Hospices de Beaune, a
charity hospital that has served the poor of the
city for more than five hundred years. The hospital's
good work continues because its founders en-
dowed it with some of the richest vineyards in the
world. To stress the medieval flavor of the fairy-tale
atmosphere, I built up the details: half-timbered,
shaped gables, etc. Drawn in a custom-made 15"
x 20" sketchbook of Glastonbury Antique drawing
paper with Faber Markettes, Winsor & Newton
watercolors and a Faber 702 sketching pencil.
From "Three Glorious Days of Burgundian Bacchanalia" for the Daily Telegraph Magazine, London,
September 17, 1971. Reproduced by permission of
the owners, Mr. and Mrs. Kenneth Twist, Cambridge, England.*

The Hôtel-Dieu · Cour d'Honneur

and for good measure, a mammoth Rabelaisian feast for the six hundred members of the Brotherhood of Burgundy Lovers at the Chateau Clos de Vougeot.

As usual with magazine journalism, there was very little time to undertake a great deal of research. I had little more than a publicity release prepared by the public relations department of a large English company of wine importers. I added a little knowledge by reading from the excellent *Guide Michelin*.

Nevertheless, the more I read about the famous old wine capital of Burgundy—with its Gothic marvels and its exuberant way of life— the more my enthusiasm began to grow for depicting my assignment in an architectural context. I was able to assemble images in my imagination, and when I actually began to work in Beaune, France, I did so with increased awareness. Not only did my research help establish the city's past, its way of life, but it also offered me all kinds of incidental ideas of how I could compose and carry out my drawings (see page 98).

Lane in the Pechersk Monastery, Kiev, U.S.S.R., 1967. *Here I used an ancient cobbled lane to help make this glimpse of old Kiev much more evocative. I used a Faber 702 graphite sketching pencil and washes of diluted Higgins India ink. The onion-shaped dome of the church in the background was filled in with a yellow marker. Drawn on Glaston-bury Antique drawing paper bound in a 15″ x 20″ custom-made sketchbook. From* A Russian Journey: from Suzdal to Samarkand, 1969. *Courtesy Cassell and Company, London; and Hill & Wang, Inc., New York.*

HOW TO DRAW YOUR SUBJECT

How I will draw a building usually depends on how much time I have. However little this may be, I usually take a good long look from two or three different positions; I can actually save time by making a firm general decision I can stay with until completion. I will return to view-points later in the chapter.

The extra work usually involved in drawing architecture can sometimes keep me pinned down to a spot for several hours. Therefore, I invariably make sure to jot down my ideas in a small pocket notebook, even if I do not feel like making the finished drawing on the particular day. I prowl around my subject, working out various alternative compositions. For example, I may heighten a particular dramatic impact of a building, place buildings against smaller, less important ones, or even add a suggestion of surrounding landscape.

The Round Tower, Kells, Ireland, 1964. *(Right) Finding an effective focal point is often the key to a successful townscape. Perched on a rise on the fringe of the town, this view seemed almost ready-made. I used a 7B Venus graphite pencil for it. Courtesy the Shelbourne Hotel, Dublin, Ireland.*

KELLS =
The ROUND TOWER
Built 10 STAIRS -

Dresden, Germany, 1960. (*Left*) *By working with different angles of light—the sun in front or behind—and by using different drawing media, mood and atmosphere can be created. This helps to express the character of architecture. For example, this ruined baroque church in Dresden, Germany was drawn in 1960 against the afternoon sun with a soft, Hardtmuth charcoal lead, and a harder Conté Pierre Noir lead for the pedimented frontage in the right foreground. In this way I was able to express more graphically the essential nobility of the classical style. An unpublished drawing from my own collection.*

The Congregational Church, Windsor, Connecticut. (*Right*) *On the other hand, this church was drawn in 1963 with the sun behind me. I used Spencerian and Gillot 303 nibs for the linear work and a Japanese brush to fill the solid areas. Thus, I was able to convey the church's puritanical severity much more effectively. Reproduced by permission of the owner, Tom Mathews, Cavendish, England.*

Sometimes I may condense a large elaborate building into a foreshortened vertical shape. I also look around for various elements or objects—such as lamp standards or fountains—which can be brought in from elsewhere and placed against a façade or an area of color. This exploratory process enables me to get "the bit between my teeth" by gradually overcoming any uncertainty or hesitation I may have about how I will actually make the drawing.

THE IMPORTANCE OF VIEWPOINT

A drawing made from an angle which best conveys the essential character of a building is generally fresher and more original to the eye. Even if the result is far from being what you first intended, finding the right angle can be the key to a successful interpretation, because it can lead to organizing your approach. Cultivate the habit of prowling around your subject. Look at it from as many angles as possible before finally committing yourself.

Ignoring perspective—which I will discuss in the next chapter—you may, as I often do, feel that a composite viewpoint would be best. It may express more cogently what you feel, condensing as it will two or even three working positions in one; in this way you can often produce a more intense interpretation. But before you attempt composite viewpoints, try out simple front views which give you plenty of practice in rendering such details as billboard advertisements, columns, entablatures, pediments, capitals, pillars, portals, signs, and windows. You have to acquire confidence that you can handle what you see. Therefore, do not attempt *too* much before you feel able to handle a large and elaborate subject.

THE BEST TIME TO DRAW

In the morning light buildings look very different than they do in afternoon or early evening

The Cockpit, Eton, England, 1968. *This vignette of the famous teashop (or "tuck" shop), a favorite rendezvous of Eton schoolboys on every occasion, was drawn in ink and watercolor in a 10¾″ x 14½″ English Planet sketchbook of smooth drawing paper. From a portfolio on Eton for* Boys' Life *magazine, November, 1971. Courtesy* Boys' Life *magazine, New York.*

PaulHOGARTH

PALMA = CONSULADO DE MAR

light. Therefore, the actual time you choose to work will depend on how you see a building. I have drawn a vast Russian monastery against a declining sun. The partially silhouetted effect that this lighting created accentuated the drama of my historical associations of the place. On the other hand, Victorian city halls and Renaissance palaces are often best drawn in the light of early morning, because this light most clearly reveals the details of their massive, extravagant ornaments.

TIME LIMITATIONS

Whether I make a relatively simple or a complicated drawing in color or black and white depends to a large extent on how many drawings I can reasonably hope to make in the time I have allotted. This is sometimes impossible to estimate, for you cannot always predict what you might discover. In this respect, ink tends to be a more deceptive and unpredictable medium than pencil, particularly when you become involved with the vast textural possibilities of, say, Victorian brickwork—a time-consuming job if you have a compulsion, as I do, to get it right.

A simple line technique, involving the use of a steel pen or brush, is the kind of drawing I am likely to make if I have only an hour or so and have to make further drawings. If I have a greater amount of time, I make a much more elaborate drawing, involving the use of color markers, watercolors, pens, and pencils. Such a drawing may take me two or three hours—even a whole morning or afternoon.

Of course, you do not have to complete a drawing on location. In fact, I often find it a good thing to finish a large ambitious drawing in my room or studio at a more leisurely pace. The important thing is to be sure you make all the necessary notes to enable you to finish the drawing when you return to your home or studio.

Consulado de Mar, Palma, Majorca, 1963. *At one time this fine old palace housed the Sea Trade Court of the island. It is now the Maritime Museum crowded with tattered flags, instruments, and memorabilia of the Barbary corsairs who once overran the Mediterranean. Drawn entirely with 3B and 7B Venus graphite pencils on Saunders paper. From Majorca Observed, 1965. Courtesy Cassell and Company, London; and Doubleday & Company, Inc., New York.*

4
Handling Perspective

Drawing architecture creatively calls for a personal response to length, width, and depth. The study of perspective as a method of depicting these three basic dimensions on a flat, or two-dimensional, surface is essential. It is necessary to find a system that will convey these dimensions and will expand the quality of your drawing.

CLASSIC WESTERN PERSPECTIVE

Most of you are familiar with at least one system of perspective; in its most basic form, this is a single horizontal line drawn across a sheet of paper. By drawing this horizontal line (in itself suggestive of the natural horizon where earth, sea, and sky appear to meet), the artist creates the illusion of space and distance. The addition of a house below the line and a cloud or two above completes the picture of earth meeting sky in the distance. If you place the house's roof so that it obscures a section of the horizon, this sets the horizon farther in the distance—behind the house.

In true perspective the natural horizon and the artist's eye level are at the same height. Whether he is lying on the ground or on the top of a skyscraper, the horizon always seems to meet his eye level with a system of parallel lines converging to a vanishing point. The only exceptions are upright lines and lines parallel to the horizon.

True, or scientific, perspective came into being as an exact science during the Renaissance. Its fundamental principles were largely worked out by the Florentine architect, Filippo Brunelleschi (1377–1446) and compiled in book form by his contemporary, the painter Paolo Uccello (1397–1475). The result of these studies was an entirely new approach to drawing which utilized combinations of architectural exteriors and interiors as settings for religious and allegorical paintings.

Alfabia, Majorca, 1963. *(Right) A timeless avenue of plane trees leads to the baroque portal of the manor of Alfabia near Bunola. This row of trees made me choose true perspective with a single vanishing point. Drawn on mold-made, cream-wove Saunders writing paper with 3B and 7B Venus graphite pencils. From* Majorca Observed, 1965. *Courtesy Cassell and Company, London; and Doubleday & Company, Inc., New York.*

Today, when the camera can undertake the more literal documentation of architecture, true perspective has much less importance for the painter and illustrator. It has much more relevance for architects, engineers, landscape specialists, and industrial designers; through the careful use of perspective, these craftsmen can show their clients the appearance of a building before it is actually constructed. But, in my opinion, earlier systems for suggesting depth, or third dimension conceived before that of Brunelleschi—used singly or in combination with one another—produce much more personal solutions to the perspective problem. They permit the artist to improvise, usually with infinitely more exciting and wider-ranging results. Let me briefly review some of the more important ones.

EARLIER PERSPECTIVE SYSTEMS

Artists have used perspective depth and distance since the Stone Age. On the walls of the great caves of Lascaux herds of horses, bison, and reindeer were etched or painted in various sizes, as if seen beyond the more fully realized animals in the foreground from the vantage point of a hill. The artists of ancient Egypt used a system of perspective which showed an object or person by combining a number of views on the same plane.

Indians of the American Northwest developed a completely different method for suggesting perspective; they showed the front view of a person, place, or animal together with both their left and right sides—as if they were split right down the middle and stretched out like a skin or hide. Chinese and Japanese artists created their illusions of depth, or perspective, by arranging the elements of land and water as a backdrop for a formal view of architecture known as isometric projection (lines are drawn

Shanghai, China, 1954. *The vast flatness of China's eastern coastal region forced me to drop conventional, true perspective and try out bird's-eye views for my graphic summations of Chinese cities. This one was made from the roof of the King Kong Hotel (formerly the Cathay). It was drawn in an hour and a half with two degrees of charcoal lead: a soft Hardtmuth and a medium hard No. 3 Conté Pierre Noir. From* Looking at China, 1955. *Courtesy Lawrence and Wishart, London, England.*

Tbilisi, Georgia, U.S.S.R., 1967. *(Right) In this drawing of the Kura section of the Georgian capital, I saw my subject as a pattern of differently-shaped elements fitting into each other like a jigsaw puzzle. Drawn in a custom-made sketchbook of English Basingwerk Antique laid drawing paper with a Faber 702 sketching pencil. From* A Russian Journey: from Suzdal to Samarkand, 1969. *Courtesy Cassell and Company, London; and Hill & Wang, Inc., New York.*

TBILISI : Re KURA
Paul MocARTA

Broad and Spring Garden Streets, Philadelphia, 1968. *This composite ink and wash drawing was based on a single horizon line with two widely separated vanishing points. The first of these is on the left with the City Hall. A second vanishing point enabled me to emphasize the huge Smith, Kline and French office block on the right. Drawn on Strathmore illustration board with Spencerian and Gillot 303 nibs and Higgins India ink. Diluted and undiluted passages of the ink were painted in with a Japanese brush. Reproduced by permission of the owners, Smith, Kline and French Laboratories, Philadelphia, Pennsylvania.*

parallel instead of converging as in "true" perspective). On the other hand, European artists of the Middle Ages used a more individual approach in which architecture was seen as a series of lively calligraphic shapes whose size was determined by the amount of space available in the margins of an illuminated manuscript.

All these systems of perspective allowed the artist to make a much less inhibited interpretation of architecture.

A PERSONAL SOLUTION

I started out using true, or classic, perspective, but it did not take me long to realize that, more often than not, the system acted as a straitjacket rather than a stimulus; it forced me to literally copy my subject. Only when I broke away from the formal rules of perspective and used the more elastic perspective systems seen in oriental paintings did I really begin to get the results I wanted.

Let me give you an example. When I was drawing Eton College for *Boys' Life* in 1968, I discovered that the visual impact of Tudor architecture increased in direct proportion to the amount you could take in at one glance. Therefore, if *several* related college buildings could be seen from above as well as from eye level, they could all add up to a much more expressive image.

I had drawn the main entrance gate—the Upper School—to School Yard, using one-point perspective at more or less eye level. But inside the gate, the vast cobblestone courtyard was filling up with boys of all shapes and sizes on their way to classes; this scene was played against the background of yet another gate—Lupton's Tower and a statue of King Henry VI, founder of the College. In my first sketch, I felt I had only nibbled at the subject. So I moved inside and added another viewpoint—more than one—and extended my drawing upwards, unrolling the entire composition like a carpet. The final result was much more animated and many-sided than would have been possible using a single point of view (see page 99).

You can use these alternate systems singly or blend them with classic perspective to create your own method of getting depth and distance into your drawing of architecture.

Building a New Skyscraper, Avenue of the Americas, New York, 1964. *Exaggerated true perspective, using one or two vanishing points on a low horizon line, can sometimes be an effective means of dramatizing a downtown city subject. Drawn entirely with a Faber 702 sketching pencil on Strathmore Script drawing paper. An unpublished drawing from my own collection.*

5
Drawing Buildings on Location

Once you are familiar with the essentials of drawing buildings, the next step is to put them into practice by working as much as possible on location.

This may not come easily at first. When I began drawing buildings on the spot, I found it difficult to remain for even half an hour and engage in what I felt was a self-conscious and solitary activity. If you, too, experience this sense of isolation, take a fellow student along and make it a joint sketching trip. This can often make all the difference to your general state of mind, your ability to put up with onlookers and possibly failure. Later, when you have acquired more self-confidence, you will feel more able to cope with everything on your own.

TAKING NOTES

Acquire the habit of carrying a small pocket-size sketchbook, a pencil, and a fiber-tip or ballpoint pen with you. This will enable you to make a scribbled note of a building—where it is, and when and how to return to it. Then you can make a more finished sketch or drawing of it at a later date.

SELECTING AND OBSERVING A BUILDING

Begin by choosing a building which not only interests you visually, but one you really feel you could draw. Moreover, make sure it is one you would enjoy drawing because of its historical or personal significance.

Too often the student of architectural drawing will take on a large and complex building without any previous consideration of how it should be depicted. Do not just sit down and copy what is in front of you. Note the fundamental shape of the building. In nature there are very few square corners, but man's most common form of construction is the box. Most

Broadway at Times Square, New York City, 1963. (*Right*) *Concentrating on a focal point, leaving out unnecessary detail, and drawing only what is strictly essential invariably increase the pace and tension of a big city subject. Drawn in an hour with a Gillot 303 nib and Higgins India ink on white Saunders paper. Originally reproduced on the jacket of* Brendan Behan's New York, 1964. *Courtesy Hutchinson Publishing Group, London; and Bernard Geis Associates, New York.*

Hollywood
old house on
Sunset Boulevard
Paul Hogarth

buildings are modifications of boxes. More-over, curved or irregular forms are more easily drawn when fitted into boxes. Try to determine the essential geometric shape of a building before you draw it.

Ask yourself how you see the building. This will help you to look for the most effective means of graphically defining its personality. Once you have even a little insight into what has aroused your interest in a building, your drawing is much more likely to succeed—to be more lively in its interpretation.

OBTAINING PERMISSION

Owners of most buildings are usually delighted that you have chosen to depict their place of residence or business. But should they appear unexpectedly on the scene, it is just as well to clear it with them before you begin. If there is an objection, all you have to emphasize is that you are simply an artist drawing purely for personal satisfaction. If publication is involved, I myself usually check to see if this is O.K.

For the majority of large buildings—whether publicly or privately owned—the problem does not arise. However, in Europe, permission is sometimes necessary to draw certain royal or privately-owned palaces and government buildings of historic interest. Under such circumstances all you need to do is ask a custodian for an official permit. Usually, these are immediately provided after payment of a small fee.

TIPS FOR WORKING ON LOCATION

When you are ready to begin working on location, start where you feel free to work undisturbed. Drawing architecture is a more complicated exercise than, say, drawing people or landscapes. I began by drawing quiet country houses simply because I knew I would go un-

House on Sunset Boulevard, Hollywood, Los Angeles, California, 1971. *Just to satisfy an old curiosity, I spent most of a day walking on Sunset Boulevard looking for the homes of silent movie stars. Near Laurel Canyon, I found this one. Affectionately drawn with Faber Markettes, Grumbacher watercolors, and a Faber 702 sketching pencil in an 11" x 14" sketchbook of Strathmore Alexis drawing paper. An unpublished drawing from my own collection.*

noticed, and I could concentrate more easily on working out the details of ornamentation.

If you feel as I did (and still do!), look around for concealed or partially concealed positions which will enable you to work in comparative peace.

EQUIPMENT

Let's go back briefly to tools, materials, and equipment. Take only what you will use that day. If you are working on a large scale, you will need a 16" × 23" sketchbook of drawing paper; if you are working on a smaller scale, 11" × 14" is a good size. You will also need soft graphite pencils, and a sharp knife; if you want to use color, you will need a box of watercolors or markers. A small, light folding stool—easily carried under your arm, or in a zippered carry-all—will enable you to sit wherever and whenever you wish.

HANDLING THE CURIOUS

It may not be possible to work entirely undisturbed! The difficulty with working on location is that people will catch sight of you—an artist drawing a well-known landmark or local building—and find it impossible to suppress their curiosity. Such interest is natural enough, and usually I do not find it unwelcome. On the contrary, it sometimes cheers me up, particularly when I am working on a big drawing which may take me two or three hours.

However, sometimes I find myself unable to take the necessary steps to prevent such curiosity from getting out of hand. My main fear is children who invariably seem to like me and set up a sort of playing field where I am working. Therefore, I always try to do my location work during the school hours, and, of course, during the week. This is particularly important in the countries of Africa, South America, or Asia where children seem to live permanently in the streets.

But there is little you can do about children during the long period of summer vacation. I remember making an unexpected trip to Fez, Morocco, in August, 1971. Everyday for one hectic week I was literally overwhelmed by children who clustered around me as though I was the Pied Piper himself. In desperation I resorted

The Cloisters, Eton College, England, 1968. *(Above) Arched doorways, bracketed lamps, cartouches, plaques, and mullioned windows enlivened this otherwise formal subject, the famous cloisters. Drawn in Pelikan Fount India ink with a Spencerian nib and a Japanese brush. From a portfolio on Eton for* Boys' Life *magazine, November, 1971. Courtesy* Boys' Life *magazine, New York.*

Botanic Gardens, Dublin, 1971. *(Right) Founded by the Royal Dublin Society in 1733 at Summerhill, the world-famous gardens are really an architectural monument. Vast collections of lushly exotic plants and vegetation are housed in elegantly designed pavilions done in classical style, all of cast iron. I used a Faber 702 sketching pencil, Faber Markettes, Winsor & Newton watercolors, and Higgins India ink with a No. 6 Winsor & Newton sable brush and a Gillot 303 nib, respectively. Drawn on an 18" x 12" sketchbook of medium smooth Daler drawing paper. From a portfolio on the Royal Dublin Society for the* Smithsonian Magazine, *August, 1971. © Smithsonian Institution, Washington, D.C.*

to subterfuge; I shrugged my shoulders in mock despair and packed my things; I would return surreptitiously a half hour later when the coast had cleared. Eventually when this—the most successful ruse—was discovered, I had to concede to the blandishments of a persistent guide or older boy; for a few dirhams he would wave a stick and shout abusive epithets to keep the numbers down and send everyone on his way.

BUILDINGS AND PEOPLE

Most buildings function as a background or center for human activity. I seldom lose the opportunity to enliven a drawing by adding single figures or a group which may move in or across my line of vision. I use such figures to heighten the mood or atmosphere of a given building or place. I usually carry two pocket-size sketchbooks (3½" × 5") for making thumbnail sketches of faces and figures and a 5" × 7" for larger groups. This material is later transferred to the large drawing in the calm of my hotel room or studio.

WHEN TO STOP

Drawing a building does not mean that you necessarily have to put everything in—starting at the top and finishing at the bottom. A certain amount of restraint is necessary. You must avoid overworking whatever you have done. You must also prevent unnecessary overemphasis which can make your drawing appear labored.

I avoid excess in my own drawings by concentrating on a focal point of architectural interest and human activity, perhaps more than one. I evolve and develop the detail from the center of the drawing, leaving the outer fringes more or less untouched. On other occasions, the subject may suggest a more decorative exploitation of shape and texture. Then I will fill up almost every inch of my drawing paper.

Canton Teahouse, China, 1954. *The ancient open-fronted teahouses of old Canton are elaborately decorated with calligraphic signs embellished with reliefs of blossom and fruit. But they are despairingly difficult to draw because of the extraordinary interest Chinese people have in watching artists at work on location. I completed this drawing from a partially covered truck after hundreds of smiling faces refused to move from my line of vision. Drawn with a Hardtmuth charcoal lead on Chinese bamboo paper. From* Looking at China, 1955. *Courtesy Lawrence and Wishart, London, England.*

6
Color and Architecture

Generally speaking, a black and white image is an essential foundation for drawing architecture. Yet color can perform an almost equally important role if used creatively. Invariably color adds a more personal and subjective quality, enabling you to intensify and heighten the total visual impact of your drawing.

DEVELOPING A PERSONAL COLOR SENSE

In architecture, as in nature, color can be *descriptive* or it can be *associative*. It can even be both. You can either translate the actual colors you see into their nearest equivalent or you can, as I frequently do, think of color as also having emotional or nostalgic significance. This type of thinking justifies using your own colors when they may not actually exist in the building you are drawing.

For example, I think of Gothic as black, rococo as turquoise, High Victorian as alizarin crimson, and 1930's "Aztec" as sepia. Cities also have colors. For me, Paris is viridian and mauve; London is silver, vermilion, and gray; and New York is green. I also have favorite colors: chrome yellow, raw siena, olive, viridian, and Payne's gray. At the risk of repeating myself, I will use these colors whenever I can. Just to have the chance of using them on a white sheet of fine drawing paper gives me pleasure.

Developing a personal sense of color also depends on your ability to edit and select—to create a color scheme out of the color you actually will see. You might begin with a more or less ambiguous color which generally dominates a building; then you can use splashes of intense color to enliven the scheme. I strongly recommend a study plan which will involve you in applying and devising color schemes. Hans Schwarz's little textbook, *Color for the Artist* (New York: Watson-Guptill; London: Studio Vista Limited) is a concise and informative outline.

HOW TO USE COLOR

To use color in an original and vital way, you must make your own experiments. When I first began to use color in drawing architecture, I tried to force color into the rigid framework of a detailed monochrome drawing. This left me with no options for using color. My mistake was to envisage a building *totally* in black and white. I did not consider color until I had completed the drawing. By that time it was too late; there was no alternative but to involve myself with the dubious practice of "coloring up" or filling in the spaces between the lines. I was using watercolor, but under these circumstances, it seemed to add nothing to the drawing. Either the color obscured the quality of my line or it was not strong enough to enliven the line. I was, in fact, placing far too much emphasis on drawing and not enough on painting, that is, thinking in color.

I finally achieved a breakthrough in 1966-7 on assignments which took me successively to Morocco, Tunisia, Libya, and Russia—countries where color is an essential part of their architectural tradition. Here I was compelled to find a new way of depicting such architecture. Fortunately, by this time the Eberhard Faber Company had introduced their high quality, revolutionary Permapoint Markettes, called Design Markettes. Faced with such a wealth of exotic architecture, I splashed about in color, often combining markers with watercolor and inks. So effectively did these color markers blend with the soft graphite line, which is the basis of my drawing style, that for the first time I felt free of my previous inhibitions and failures with color. To use color creatively you must adapt your drawing so that color can become an effective and integral part of it.

COMBINING COLOR AND LINE

Color should be introduced into your drawing as soon as possible. When I made my mixed media color drawing, *Grauman's Chinese Theater, Hollywood, 1971* (page 103), I kept my initial 3B pencil outline to a minimum. Then, after having referred to my preliminary color notes and composition, I quickly plunged in with a chrome yellow marker. I filled in the entire overall shape of the building just as a painter would establish an underpainting. Later I painted over this yellow with a translucent, blotted wash of raw siena to create a solid yet luminous effect.

Then, I worked alternately in pencil and color, developing the detail of a section here and a section there, painting in the freely drawn pencil shapes with scattered spots of crimson, gold, and orange. I had moments of anxiety until I could relate the pencil with the color. I did this by deploying large shapes—such as the luxuriant green climbing plant. This plant acted as a foil to the sharply delineated pencil detail of a host of dragons which embellished the roof above the restaurant's entrance. Finally, I added a selection of the most graphic footprints, handprints, legprints, and inscriptions in the concrete which are so much a part of the world-famous Hollywood theater. Such details can add to a building's ambiance.

MAKING COLOR NOTES

You must be able to visualize a color before you can mix it. You cannot make a drawing or paint a picture in your head. Therefore, I make color notes on my compositional sketch. These notes enable me to see color much more analytically. Before I began the watercolor drawing, *The Rooftops of Beaune* (page 98) I had a very clear idea of how I would handle the color almost to the last brushstroke. My notes were precise and informative so if I did not have the time to complete what was a large finished picture, I could recollect the colors when I was back in my studio.

I particularly noted delicate or subtle hues, and of course, any special details which characterized certain buildings, like the color of a pinnacle (a slender decorative tower found in Gothic architecture) or a cupola, or a dome. I also reminded myself of any textural effects which would enrich my drawing—like a diluted India ink wash over a band of more or less solid color. I scribbled such notes hastily with one eye on my watch, but I never for one moment regretted having done so. They are personal reminders; they are as vital as a sailing chart to a yachtsman sailing in unfamiliar waters.

So, look hard at your subject before you begin. Identify its *hue*, or the quality which distinguishes one color from another; its *tone*, or degree of light or dark; and finally, its *strength*, or saturation. The stronger or more brilliant a color is, the greater its intensity. Describe these qualities precisely and in as few words as possible. Not only will these notes help you to become more aware of color, but they will increase your facility to work with it.

Page from My Beaune Notebook. (Above) It was November and bitterly cold. I could not stand working for more than an hour or so. Color notes scribbled over my composition sketch enabled me to complete the watercolor painting The Rooftops of Beaune in the warmth of my hotel room (see page 98, color section). I used similar color notes for the drawing on the opposite page.

Sunday Morning on the Cochrane Ranch, Alberta, Canada, 1969. (Right) A barn should possess its own identity as a piece of rural vernacular architecture. Part of a barn's identity (at least in the United States) is integrally related to its color—"barn" red. I contrasted the red of the barn with the yellow-green of the grassy field in the foreground. This luxuriant grass and the cowhand set off and highlight the barn's blistered, weather-beaten exterior. Drawn in two hours with a Faber 702 sketching pencil, Faber Design Markettes, and Winsor & Newton watercolors in a custom-made 15" x 20" sketchbook of Glastonbury Antique drawing paper. Reproduced by permission of the owners, Mr. and Mrs. Kenneth Twist, Cambridge, England.

SOME RANDOM HINTS

The basic ingredient of drawing architecture as such is a calligraphic line. Try to restrict yourself to those colors which blend effectively with ink, brush, or pencil—the traditional linear media. I say restrict advisedly, because the range of media that produce a line is wide and includes felt-tip markers, watercolors, gouache, colored inks, pastels, crayons, and colored pencils.

Broadly speaking, I have found the most successful color medium to be that which is transparent such as felt-tip markers, watercolors, and colored inks. All these can produce rich, intense, and glowing colors which are difficult to equal in opaque media such as gouache or acrylic. Of course, there is no reason why this rule should not be broken and why you should not experiment with both opaque and transparent colors and combine them with one another.

COLOR MARKERS

Because they combine drawing with painting, felt-tip markers are God's own gift if you have hangups about using color in your drawings. I strongly recommend their use as the first step in handling color in relation to drawing. Markers are an ideal medium with which to start your explorations of color in relation to architecture.

You may find, as I did, that pure colors—particularly blues, browns and reds—require careful handling; otherwise they can obliterate a pencil line. Get used to the hues and tones of a basic color range of yellow, orange, red, blue-violet, blue, blue-green, green and yellow-green; use the solid pure colors sparingly.

Markers are also useful for making quick color sketches and for noting down details relating to color if you do not have the time to complete a drawing. They also work equally well as a foundation for patches, washes, or tints of watercolor or ink washes (see my drawing, *Cathedral of St. Basil,* page 100). They also work well by themselves with soft graphite pencil, charcoal pencil, or leads.

Markers have a fascination, it seems, for children as well as artists. When I was in Samarkand, U.S.S.R. I did a drawing of the Shah-i-Zinda mosques. I decided to use markers as well as watercolors to capture the warm orange, and yellows of the ancient buildings. However, this ancient monument now stays in my mind as the place where a nine-year-old boy, unable to hold out any longer, made off with the whole box of Faber Markettes!

WATERCOLOR

The transparent qualities of watercolor have always made it an ideal medium for drawing architecture. I am speaking of a watercolor *drawing* rather than a watercolor *painting* (see my drawing *Art Nouveau Apartment House, Moscow, 1967,* page 102).

I avoid making too detailed a drawing before starting to use watercolor. I use a method which relies almost entirely on a semi-finished drawing (usually in pencil) and fill it in with watercolor washes. Sometimes the pencil line shows through. I do not mind; it adds to the personal flavor of my drawing. Sometimes I will make a much less complete drawing in pencil before using color and work on a foundation that is filled in with a pastel or light-color marker.

GOUACHE

Pencil or ink also works well with gouache, or solid opaque color. Gouache is a watercolor bound with gum. It is quick-drying and if it is required, additional layers or touches of paint can be applied quickly. There is, however, the danger that these opaque colors will flake off if mixed too thickly. Gouache can be bought in jars or tubes and are known as poster or designer's colors. You can also—as I sometimes do—simply put a tube of Chinese white and lamp black in your color box and add them to your own watercolors to give them the necessary opacity.

I hardly ever make a complete color drawing with gouache. That is, I never work pure gouache against gouache. I use gouache more to achieve textural effects that necessitate an opaque color over a transparent one, or vice versa. I sometimes simulate a discolored surface or wall by blotting a gouache wash. This blotting action disperses, or curdles, the pigment

COLORED INKS

Colored inks are inclined to encourage you to use color boldly, particularly if you use them on a stylized or decorative type of drawing made in black India ink. Used in this way, straight from the bottle, colored inks can produce intense effects reminiscent of medieval stained glass.

Being waterproof, artist's quality colored inks can be applied in successive layers, without producing the tired, muddy look of several layers of watercolor. I also use colored inks in mixed media drawings where I need a scattered spot of pure intense color.

PASTELS, CRAYONS, AND COLORED PENCILS

I have made a few drawings with pastels (particularly the superb Dutch Rembrandt Artists Pastels). But for me, a traveling artist, pastels are an impractical color medium. Despite their well-made boxes with felt or wool-lined channels to hold every stick, they are not easy to carry without damaging them. Nothing is more maddening than to find the pastel sticks you need broken into two, three, or even more fragments. Pastels are very fragile and should really only be used in the studio. Drawings done with them are liable to smudge and dust off. Moreover, fixative, while preventing them from smudging, seems to deaden their purity.

Pastels work best with a scribbly texture rather than a solid filled-in technique. They combine well with a soft graphite, or better still, charcoal lead. Pastel drawings should be placed under glass or plastic film as soon as possible.

Wax crayons, or oil pastels as they are called, are more vivid than traditional pastels. They are cheaper too! Again, they are a medium which looks best when used in a bold and open style, avoiding the use of solid color.

On the other hand, colored pencils permit greater detail. These pencils, like wax crayons, depend for their color on a strongly graphic concept in black and white to be effective.

Shah-i-Zinda, Samarkand, U.S.S.R., 1967. (*Next Page*) *The mosques and mausoleums of this unique complex were built in the fourteenth century by the Emperor Tamurlane who chose Samarkand (the name means "fruit and sugar") as the site for his capital. The warm yellows and oranges that I used on the buildings suggests their natural color while enhancing the ambiance of opulence that their history evokes. The viridian of the hillside forms a cool contrast to these warm colors. Drawn with a Faber 702 sketching pencil, Faber Design Markettes, and Soviet watercolors on a double-page spread of a custom-made 15" x 20" sketchbook of English Glastonbury Antique drawing paper. From A Russian Journey: from Suzdal to Samarkand, 1969. Courtesy Cassell and Company, London; and Hill & Wang, Inc., New York.*

Paul Hogarth. The Mausoleums of Shah-
Zinda, SAMARKAND

7
Drawing Castles and Fortresses

My childhood reading, together with the movies, created an image of castles and fortresses of every kind as the most romantically tragic examples of historical architecture. Indeed, they have long been a favorite subject for most artists. I am thinking of the sublime ruins of Turner, of the sun-scorched fortresses of Edward Lear, and the sinister strongholds of Gustave Doré. Closer to our own time are the mythical watchtowers of Arthur Rackham and Maxfield Parrish, and the fantastic baronial follies of John Glashan.

CASTLES THROUGHOUT HISTORY

Perched like sentinels above swirling rivers, at the junctions of lonely roads, or the approaches to a distant valley, these ancient and time-ravaged buildings are found almost everywhere in Europe and North Africa, long battlegrounds of warring nations. Fortresses were built by various Mediterranean peoples several thousand years before the Christian era, but it was the Byzantines who developed castle-building into an art. Castles and fortresses spread to Western Europe in the ninth century. At first, they were simple defensive points of earthworks and wooden palisades. Then, during the eleventh century the Normans invaded England and built these defenses with stone.

The Normans who were particularly active castle builders were especially so in England. Many of their castles still stand and can be found throughout the country. The grim, massive Tower of London with its square keep, or *donjon*, is a splendid example of such a building; it was one of my first castle drawings.

The Talipoch Gate, Bukhara, U.S.S.R., 1967. *(Right) Sheep graze by the ancient walls of this city built over twelve centuries ago. I began the drawing by making a pencil outline, then painting the gate and walls directly with a fully loaded brush and diluted and undiluted passages of Winsor & Newton watercolor. Here and there I allowed parts to dry in order to simulate flaking or pitted textures. Then I laid in a flat pale wash—which I quickly blotted to avoid running—to convey solidity. The road off to the right and the main highway in the foreground were painted in with a diluted blotted wash of Higgins India ink. The sheep, the shepherd, and the Soviet jeep were drawn with a Faber 702 sketching pencil. Drawn for* A Russian Journey: from Suzdal to Samarkand *but not published.*

Bukhara: the Talipach Gate

The Great Wall of China near Chinglungchiao, China, 1954. *I remember looking upon the wrinkled hills and rugged mountains, over which the mighty Wall plunged and twisted as far as the eye could see. Eagles flew above and below a train of belled dromedaries plodded on with tireless patience. I bathed in the historic atmosphere and relaxed before the tranquil panorama beneath my feet. Drawn with a medium Hardtmuth charcoal lead on Abbey Mill drawing paper. An unpublished drawing from my trip to China in 1954.*

Throughout the Middle Ages (from the eleventh to the fourteenth centuries), castles grew larger. They evolved their own community life and social organization. In time of trouble castles provided refuge for the local populace. They were also the residence of the feudal nobility and administrative center for baronial or royal government. Medieval cities also had castles within their walls. Some cities were (as were palaces and monasteries) surrounded by complex systems of turreted walls, rounded watchtowers, sloping buttresses, drawbridges, gate houses, and large deep moats.

THE END OF CASTLES

Eventually, castles were made obsolete by firearms and gunpowder. They also fell out of favor as residences because the nobility demanded greater comforts within the privacy of a country estate. At first, castles were gradually replaced by great houses which incorporated defensive features, such as battlements, secret passages, and watchtowers. These great houses were followed by a proliferation of halls, courts, and ducal palaces designed by architects usually in the grand or classical manner.

Only with the Romantic revival in the late eighteenth and early nineteenth centuries did the castle come into its own again as a residence. This revival frequently produced splendidly bogus edifices of great style, such as the Royal Palace at Neuschwanstein, Germany (erected for Louis II of Bavaria), or Olana Castle at Catskill up the Hudson River, New York. Older castles, as at Windsor, England, were also revamped to make them more suitable for living and to create the impression of feudal splendor.

FORTRESSES AND FORTIFIED BUILDINGS

Before stone castles were built, fortified lines surrounded cities and military posts. The Romans protected whole regions with continuous ramparts interspersed with forts and towers; an example is Hadrian's Wall in the north of England. Even more spectacular is the Great Wall of China, built against the marauding Huns in the third century, B.C.

For most of the Middle Ages castles predominated. But the discovery of gunpowder

The Walls of Constantinople. *After fifteen centuries, the walls of Constantinople still stand! My assignment for Time-Life Books was to depict life in the twelfth-century capital of the Byzantine Empire. I was able to draw many of my subjects on location. In this unused illustration of the Marble Tower, an important junction of Theodosia's massive defense system is seen in good condition. I only had to add the sentries to create a twelfth-century flavor. Faber 702 sketching pencils, sharpened to chisel and fine points, helped me define the walls' structure, color, and texture more expressively. Courtesy Time, Inc., New York.*

Alcudia, Majorca, 1963. *Alcudia was formerly defended from the attacks of the Barbary corsairs by towers and ramparts which encircle the town. Now only the gateways of these fortifications remain. Drawn with a 7B Venus graphite pencil on Saunders paper. From Majorca Observed, 1965. Courtesy Cassell and Company, London; and Doubleday & Company, Inc., New York.*

during the fourteenth century created a need for more specialized military architecture of even greater proportions. Thus, the fortress, or citadel, came into being reaching its peak of perfection in seventeenth-century France.

DRAWING FORTRESSES

Fortresses have, therefore, a much more functional style. Although they may be much less romantic to draw, their extraordinary look of apparent impregnability can produce some striking subjects for your pencil.

I remember drawing the *Boy Nord*, or the Saadienne fortress, which guards the northern approaches to the Moroccan city of Fez. Built in 1532 on a rocky precipice with multicolored, time-encrusted walls, it was a fortress in every sense. I sat directly beneath the central point of its star-shaped plan, looking up at its battlements and smooth, sloping walls. The arched loopholes peered down at me like eyes and made me feel how truly formidable a task it must have been to attack the place.

WHERE TO FIND THEM

If you can possibly do so, start with Europe, selecting a single region—*not* a country—to work in. For in themselves, the Rhineland (Germany), Bohemia (Czechoslovakia), Wales (Great Britain), Muscovy (Russia) and Castile (Spain) each have more than enough castles, fortresses, or fortified cities to keep a regiment of artists busy for the entire summer.

I have found that such cities as Carcassonne (France), Suzdal (Russia), and Avila (Spain) have enough to keep me busy for much more time than I usually have.

BEGINNING YOUR DRAWING

Before succumbing to the spell exercised by your chosen castle or fortress, identify your reactions to what you see. This will enable you to draw your subject more easily.

To savor the full impact of the place and any particular historical association it may possess, I usually pretend I am an attacking soldier and begin at the entrance gate. Sometimes I walk around the castle or fortress to observe more of its general layout and any

The Spaso-Yefimovrsky Monastery, Suzdal, U.S.S.R., 1967. *Actually a vast fortress, the high walls of the Spaso-Yefimovrsky Monastery enclose dark secrets. Catherine the Great turned part of it into a prison for political incorrigibles. Here was a chance to express my own personal feelings about imprisonment, and I sought to hint at the darkness which lay behind the beauty of its exterior. I worked mainly with watercolor using a pointed Japanese brush; I used diluted and undiluted, blotted washes of color, heightened with Faber Markettes. The flocks of crows and ravens were drawn with a fully charged brush of Higgins Eternal India ink and blotted. Strangely enough, those crows in the far distance were done with a crow quill pen. Drawn in over two and a half hours across a double-page spread of a custom-made 15″ x 20″ sketchbook of Basingwerk Antique drawing paper. From A Russian Journey: from Suzdal to Samarkand, 1969. Courtesy Cassell and Company, London; and Hill & Wang, Inc., New York.*

points of unusual architectural interest. Usually these are centered around the most vulnerable point, the gatehouse which is surrounded by towers and thicker loopholed walls. At this time I decide whether I should draw a part— such as the drawbridge leading to the gatehouse and possibly on to the keep—or whether in the interests of conveying dramatic ambiance, I should attempt a more generalized view of the whole.

COMPOSING YOUR DRAWING

Castles and fortresses are sometimes so immense and complex that it is difficult to contain them within the limits of any sketchbook. Yet, there are occasions when the selection of only a part of their awesome monumentality seems to be an admission of defeat.

When making my drawing of the Spasso-Yefimovsky Monastery at Suzdal, Russia, in 1967 I found one solution. The monastery, barely visible from the outside, is completely encircled by a rose brick wall 3,600 feet long; it has cone-shaped watchtowers all around and a vast central gateway sixty feet high. It was like being faced with drawing ten blocks of New York's East Side.

I was using large sketchbooks on my Russian travels, sometimes working over two pages to give me more space (20″ × 30″). Even so, I obviously had to devise some way to enable me to get the whole structure in. Otherwise, how could I convey the enormity of the Monastery's dark secrets? Catherine the Great turned part of the monastery into a prison for her political opponents. Anticipating more recent Russian history, these opponents were declared to be "madmen" who needed the "peace" of monastic seclusion to recover their "reason." But once inside, they were never seen again.

By first concentrating on the gatehouse with its two flanking octagonal watchtowers, barbican, and buttressed walls, I solved the problem of capturing the enormity of the structure. Then, I moved to a second position and foreshortened the greater part of its high loopholed walls and watchtowers to a vanishing point sharply receding to the far horizon. Finally, to accentuate the inherently tragic atmosphere as well as the structure's vast size, I added hundreds of crows and ravens; these birds wheeled above the walls and watchtowers like the living embodiment of the unfortunate men and women who had died there.

8
The Grand Manner

During the seventeenth and eighteenth centuries civilized society was rapidly changing. Man as the measure of all things and as the creator of himself and of a developing social reality prevailed. This age of exploration and trade reaped one of Europe's great harvests of prosperity. The Spanish and the Portuguese ranged the New World for gold and converts; the Dutch, the English, and the French sought new lands for trade and settlement. Even Russia traded and thrust herself into the modern world.

The enormous profits from this trade brought a striking transformation of living standards. Newly successful merchants and the princes who collaborated with them built lavishly and well. The new nobility wanted a background style in the grand manner for their life. Country houses were built with magnificently landscaped gardens and parks. For the first time, a sense of space was introduced; the grand scale of Roman planning with its axial views and piazzas was a source of inspiration for new cities like Dublin, Philadelphia, and St. Petersburg. Palaces, government buildings, and institutions of higher education were built as architectural ensembles. Squares and vistas supplanted narrow winding streets. Dignified terraces formed the town houses of the wealthy and professional classes.

WHAT IS THE GRAND MANNER?

Architecture of the Grand Manner is, as the term implies, mannerist and *grand*. A derivative of Greek and Roman forms, this architecture evolved out of the Renaissance to embrace a whole group of styles, consecutively known as Palladian classical, baroque, rococo and neo-

The Cameron Gallery, Pushkin, U.S.S.R., 1967. *(Right) On a crisp, Russian spring day the strains of Mozart could be heard from the school of music in the nearby Catherine Palace in Pushkin. Perhaps it was just my imagination but, nevertheless, I felt it helped me delineate Charles Cameron's austere and superbly elegant gallery—his first commission for the autocratic Catherine the Great. Drawn entirely with a Faber 702 sketching pencil with touches of diluted Pelikan Fount India ink wash on Glastonbury Antique laid drawing paper. From A Russian Journey: from Suzdal to Samarkand, 1969. Courtesy Cassell and Company, London; and Hill & Wang, Inc., New York.*

Puskhin: The Cameron Gallery
Paul HOGARTH.

The Stock Exchange with Rostral Column, Pushkin Square, Leningrad, U.S.S.R., 1967. *The Grand Manner can be overwhelmingly complex, particularly in Leningrad. For example, this striking ensemble of richly ornamented lighthouses—known as the Rostral Columns—were adorned with sculptured figures and replicas of ships' prows. The scene also included the huge classical style building, the former Stock Exchange. I devised a cruciform arrangement which enabled me to make an effective image of one of the columns superimposed as a vertical shape on the horizontal shape of the Exchange. Drawn in mixed media—pencil, watercolor, and markers—in a custom-made 15" x 20" sketchbook of Glastonbury Antique laid drawing paper. From A Russian Journey: from Suzdal to Samarkand, 1969. Courtesy Cassell and Company, London; and Hill & Wang, Inc., New York. Reproduced by permission of the owner, Ruth Boswell, London, England.*

classical. Each of these styles is divided into periods and sub-styles in Italy, France, England, and Germany. For example, English Georgian and the colonial style of North America stem from neoclassical.

PRELIMINARY STUDY

In drawing the Grand Manner, the essential classical qualities of order and formal beauty should be interpreted with a large degree of exactitude. The word *classical* virtually means perfect. Without due awareness of the proportion and relationship of one item to another —such as columns and entablatures—your drawing will not succeed in capturing these classical qualities.

On the other hand, do not devote *too* much attention to getting every detail perfect. If you lose the relaxed fluency of your drawing, the result is likely to be devoid of all vitality. Carried out in the winter, preparatory study, therefore, followed by summer location work can provide a vital and basic prelude.

Borrow or buy a good historical guide to architectural style and ornament. Pothorn's *Styles of Architecture* and Meyer's *Handbook of Ornament* (now available as a Dover paperback) will tell you all you need to know and provide you with more than enough illustrations. Get thoroughly acquainted with the capitals and entablatures of the four basic classical orders: Doric, Ionic, Corinthian, and Composite. Make freehand pencil sketches of these orders and every kind of classical ornament— including animal, plant, and human forms, vase forms, and trophies of war and hunting. Keep in mind, for example, that the Corinthian capital is based on the acanthus (a species of the thistle) which was one of the principal decorative motifs of the Grand Manner. Copy all of the classical orders at first, then try to draw them fluently and naturally.

Seek out a classical or classical-style building in your neighborhood. If one does not exist, an imitation colonial style bank or church will do. Use a 3B or 6B graphite pencil to evolve a composition based on a section of the building. This need not be more than an arch, an entrance portal, a pair of gates to a house, or a church tower, but it will enable you to focus on the essentials of the classical idiom.

The more you draw, the sooner you will discover that such preliminary study helps you face larger subjects with much more confidence. Also this practice will move you closer to the lively, authoritative interpretation necessary for this type of architecture.

PLACES TO BEGIN

The next step is to look around for locations to enable you to acquire experience drawing the various classical idioms of the Grand Manner. Country houses are best; they are a delight to draw. Moreover, you can make as many mistakes as you like. The chances are that no one will be looking over your shoulder!

You do not have to visit Europe. The eastern and southern United States, and eastern Canada, provide hunting grounds almost as rich, as do the older suburbs of San Francisco and Chicago. Of course, in these cities, such houses will not be authentic but imitations. The American Automobile Association's *Tour Book* series, state by state, lists those buildings which can be visited, as do the excellent regional Mobil Travel Guides (Simon & Schuster paperbacks).

If you live in Europe or plan to visit there, Great Britain and Ireland have the greatest number of stately homes open to the public. The Automobile Association's excellent *Castles, Houses and Gardens,* available from A.A. offices throughout the United Kingdom, lists over 1,630 from Cornwall to the north of Scotland, including Wales, Northern Ireland, and the Republic of Ireland.

COUNTRY HOMES

The more successful of my earliest Grand Manner drawings were of country houses. After living in London for some years, I moved to Essex in the early 1950's and lived in an eighteenth-century house at Little Maplestead, and another at Stansfield, near Bury St. Edmunds, Suffolk. The beauty and style of both houses were a constant source of delight to live with. The result was that I found myself becoming increasingly fond of the period, especially after spending the summer of 1959 traveling about Ireland, making drawings for a book, *Brendan Behan's Island.*

The Spassky Gate, Red Square, Moscow, 1967. *The Spassky Gate is the main entrance to the Kremlin and lies on the eastern wall. Massively red, the six-teenth-century Gothic clock tower straddles an earlier gateway dating back to the Middles Ages. To emphasize the contrast of styles, I included a handsome eighteenth-century palace, part of the Kremlin complex of magnificent medieval and classical buildings. My surface was a 15″ x 20″ sketchbook of Glastonbury Antique drawing paper. Winsor & Newton watercolors with Nos. 4, 6, and 8 sable brushes were used. Faber Markettes, used over and under watercolor passages, enriched the color. An unpublished drawing from my trip to the U.S.S.R. in 1967. Reproduced by permission of the owners, Mr. and Mrs. Kenneth Twist, Cambridge, England.*

Westport House, County Mayo, Ireland, 1959. *(Left) Luxuriantly overgrown gardens can provide a setting for gracious old mansions everywhere. They particularly enhance the rational severity of the eighteenth-century classical style of this house. Drawn with Conté Pierre Noir, No. 3 charcoal lead. I used an ordinary graphite pencil as a ruler for the main lines of the house. From Brendan Behan's Island, 1962. Courtesy Hutchinson Publishing Group, London; and Bernard Geis Associates, New York.*

The Gardens of Raxa, Majorca, 1963. *(Above) In a verdant setting of cypress trees and terraced hillsides, sleeping lions, goddesses of love, urns, and fountains offered an unforgettable exercise in evoking mood. Drawn with 3B, 5B, and 6B Eagle Charco pencils on white mold-made, cream-wove Saunders writing paper. From Majorca Observed, 1965. Courtesy Cassell and Company, London; and Doubleday & Company, Inc., New York. Reproduced by permission of the owner, Dr. Louis Castor, Philadelphia, Pennsylvania.*

DUBLIN - UPPER MOUNT STREET FROM MERRION SQUARE

Ireland is so rich in the style of the Grand Manner that although our book was about the Irish and their ways, I longed to do a few examples of the Irish Grand Manner of the Adam period (1728-92). But could I persuade Brendan Behan, ex-IRA man and self-confessed opponent of the Anglo-Irish establishment, to agree? To my surprise, he was in full agreement. "Ah yes," he quipped dreamily, "the gentle people, they lived in great style; some still do, bejesus. They're as much a part of the 'ould sod as I am meself. Paul, me boyo, gie us a few drowin's of those fine plaices."

One such fine "plaice" was Westport House, the Marquis of Sligo's ancestral home at Westport, County Mayo. It seemed an indulgence to draw it, but looking back I now realize that this drawing was an exercise which helped me over the difficult hurdle of depicting the classical idiom. The strange, haunting beauty of the house literally compelled me to draw it.

Designed by Richard Cassells and James Wyatt, the house dated from 1730. It was situated in a luxuriantly overgrown desmesne (land adjoining a mansion). This overgrown shrubbery provided an idyllic setting for the house's symmetric planning, sash windows, and pedimented façades. Ivy and Virginia creeper entwined themselves around garden vases and time-encrusted statues. Overgrown grasses concealed the gentle rustling of pheasants and partridges. Under its spell, I unpacked my sketchbook and what followed was as much an illustration of the experience as it was a drawing of the house.

Whatever your reaction to the Grand Manner may be, accept it and use it as a motivating factor. Thus, you will be able to fully convey the character of your subject.

THE GRAND MANNER AND THE URBAN SCENE

When I went back to Dublin from County Mayo, I looked at the town houses of this

Upper Mount Street from Merrion Square, Dublin, 1968. *I used the domed "pepperbox" church of St. Paul as a focal point for this vista of Upper Mount Street with its banks of dignified Georgian brick houses. Drawn on Saunders paper with 3B and 7B Venus graphite pencils. Courtesy the Shelbourne Hotel, Dublin, Ireland.*

Georgian House in Harcourt Terrace, Dublin, 1964. *The south side of St. Stephen's Green abounds with elegant Georgian mansions. This one in Harcourt Terrace with its proud Ionic colonnade faces the modern world with stoic calm. Drawn with 6B and 7B Venus graphite pencils on Saunders mold-made, cream-wove writing paper. Courtesy the Shelbourne Hotel, Dublin, Ireland.*

Henrietta Street with King's Inn Library, Dublin, 1969. *The grandeur that was Dublin is nowadays a setting for a street life reminiscent of O'Casey and Behan at their best. Somehow this tumult enlivens the sober, dignified façades of the Georgian style. Drawn with a Faber 702 sketching pencil in an 11″ x 14″ sketchbook of Strathmore Alexis paper. Reprinted from Lithopinion 16. © 1969 by Local One, Amalgamated Lithographers of America, New York.*

The Main Quadrangle, Trinity College, Dublin, 1969. *To the left of this impressive scene there is the classical façade of the Examination Hall, and opposite it is the Chapel which also has a portico with a Corinthian colonnade. In the center of the cobbled square is the Campanile, a graystone bell tower, which provided an opportunity for some good, vigorous drawing. Because it was such a strong element in an otherwise dignified setting, I allowed it to dominate the cross-like composition. Even then, I felt the figures of students walking to and from their lectures were necessary to further enliven the scene. Drawn in pencil and ink wash with a Faber 702 sketching pencil and diluted Pelikan Fount India ink applied with a No. 6 Winsor & Newton sable brush. Reprinted from Lithopinion 16. © 1969 by Local One, Amalgamated Lithographers of America, New York.*

Grand Manner period with renewed interest. They took their places in ensembles of streets and squares, but they evoked reflections of an entirely different way of life.

In Dublin today there are still whole districts of eighteenth-century houses with rarely a modern building to break up their alignment. Some of these houses are well preserved with painted porches and delicately traced fanlights. Yet these same homes are flanked by others in almost derelict condition. Through open doors you can see molded plaster ceilings by James and Robert Adam crumbling above wrought-iron banisters and rotting paneling. Yet, somehow or another the lively, though impoverished, tenants of these houses seem to belong to this grand setting.

I have drawn Georgian houses and terraces in Mountjoy Square and in Henrietta Street simply because the very intensity of Dublin street life—with its gangs of laughing children, street vendors, and gossiping housewives—turns back the pages of time and gives a glimpse of what the eighteenth century must have been like.

THE CHALLENGE OF SCALE

Leningrad, or St. Petersburg as the city was originally called, has vast open spaces, immense palaces, academic institutions, government offices, and monumental edifices. These are not subjects to be depicted by the half-hearted.

Determined to gain access to the Baltic, Peter the Great, after whom the city was named, in 1703 began building a European-style city with the help of an international team of outstanding architects. No eighteenth-century city grew so quickly, or at such cost. Now the city is, perhaps, a little out of place in this century of the Common Man.

DEVELOPING A PERSONAL RESPONSE

Fortunately, my previous acquaintance with the classical style in Ireland and Spain provided me with some clues to the interpretation of some of Leningrad's Grand Manner.

One such clue was the variety of edifices or monuments which could be effectively juxtaposed against a building. Along the river Neva, near Pushkin Square, I came to the spit of Vasilevsky Island with the remarkable Rostral Columns (a pair of column-shaped lighthouses which served as beacons for ships going up the Neva). Mighty sculptural figures portraying Russia's trade routes—the Neva, the Volkov, the Volga, and the Dnieper—sat at the foot of the orange marble Rostral Columns which were also adorned with ships prows, symbols of navigation, and the elements.

I selected one column, drawing it in mixed media (pencil, watercolor, and markers). I placed it the full length of the sheet. The vast former stock exchange which was done in the Palladian-classical style lay immediately behind the column, two hundred yards away. I pushed this building into the distance of my drawing with tramlines that traveled horizontally. I moved the column to completely dominate my composition and complete the contrast of vertical against horizontal and of color against black and white.

Classical architecture in the Grand Manner can be extremely formal and dignified in almost any kind of context. To do it full justice, you have to sometimes impose your own compositional solution in order to reveal its inherent drama. To sum up, drawing the Grand Manner should be your personal comment on a way of life long since gone.

9
Ecclesiastical Architecture

Ecclesiastical architecture—churches, chapels, monasteries, synagogues, temples, mosques, and pagodas—can be inspiring, even disturbing, subjects to draw. When you look at a French Gothic cathedral, a Russian monastery, a Moroccan mosque, or a Chinese pagoda, you see an architecture which owes everything to an irrational faith; it is this faith which has extended the architecture to its absolute limits. Such buildings were designed to dominate the consciousness of man.

CAPTURING SPIRITUAL ESSENCE

I experienced the power of ecclesiastical architecture as never before during my travels in the Soviet Union in 1967 with Alaric Jacob. After a fast ride on a gleaming new electric train, we reached Vladimir, some 120 miles northeast of Moscow. Suddenly, we entered the past. On the escarpment above the railway station stood the white-walled Kremlin with the Uspensky Cathedral at its highest point. In the twelfth century this cathedral was the seat of the patriarch of the Russian Church, and the principality of Vladimir-Suzdal was the capital of the country, long before Moscow was built.

However, Vladimir today is fast becoming an industrial city. On the other hand, Suzdal is something very different. It is medieval in essence and has been preserved very much as it was in the days of Alexander Nevsky, Prince of Vladimir. Forty churches and almost as many monasteries and almshouses form an immense state historical museum. Walking through the cobbled streets of the once holy city, I felt stifled by its darkly fanatical ambiance. The clergy had departed their picturesque churches and brooding monasteries long ago, but the buildings still stand as strong as ever—build-

The Rozhdestvensky Cathedral, Suzdal, U.S.S.R., 1967. *(Right) After the Pokrovsky Convent, the Rozhdestvensky Cathedral seemed a light and carefree place without any of the hangups of the Russian past. Its walls were dazzlingly white; I dramatized this whiteness by using light gray watercolor for the cast shadows. I added the hovering ravens and peasant woman with a Gillot 303 pen and Higgins India ink. From* A Russian Journey: from Suzdal to Samarkand, 1969. *Courtesy Cassell and Company, London; and Hill & Wang, Inc., New York.*

Paul Hogarth
Suzdal: The Rozdestuensky
Cathedral

Dutch Reformed Church, Hyde Park, New York, 1963. *I always try to bring out the character of the religion itself when drawing churches or chapels. Here I used a formal setting of pine tree, path, and notice board to illustrate the no-nonsense austerity of nonconformist Protestantism. Pelikan watercolors were used plus 4B and 6B Venus graphite pencils on Saunders paper. Reproduced by permission of the owner, Jane Mull, New York.*

The Pechersk Monastery, Kiev, U.S.S.R., 1967. *The hand of the prolific Rastrelli, Catherine the Great's favorite foreign architect, is discernible in the Pechersk complex of churches and monasteries. Drawn entirely on Glastonbury Antique paper with a well-pointed clutch of 3B Venus graphite pencils plus, of course, a Faber 702 sketching pencil. Pale washes of Higgins India ink were painted on the trees to hint of the coming spring. From* A Russian Journey: from Suzdal to Samarkand, *1969. Courtesy Cassell and Company, London; and Hill & Wang, Inc., New York.*

ings of unique and unusual beauty, rising above the wooden cabins of the peasants. For example, there was the sinister Prokrovsky Monastery with its cathedral and archbishop's palace. Founded in 1364, it was used by tsars and noble families as a place to dump errant wives and unwanted children. However, I did not have to know this to be disturbed by the monastery's strange, leaning bell towers and onion-shaped cupolas. But the additional information provided by a talkative guide certainly imbued the building with even more drama.

Just as soon as I was able, I started drawing Suzdal as though I had been an eyewitness to its turbulent history. In front of the Prokrovsky Monastery I worked like one possessed, as though I had to express my own revulsion with its barbarous and *unholy* past. Therefore, it was hardly surprising that the watercolor drawing I did was one of my most successful.

CHURCHES AND CATHEDRALS

Of course, Christianity, like any other faith, has its lighter and more positive aspects. The Hôtel Dieu, or House of God, in Beaune, France, is a fine example of medieval Gothic and Romanesque architecture embellished with a vast multicolored tile roof. After the "sinister" monasteries of old Muscovy, it seemed to me a happy example of ecclesiastical architecture. For over five hundred years it has been home to the aged poor of the Burgundian wine capital. It is partly financed by the Church, but most of the money for its upkeep comes from the sale of fine wines from vineyards donated by Nicolas Rolin, Louis XI's tax collector. "He has ruined the people," said the King, "so it is fitting that he should provide them with an almshouse." The Church blessed such charity by providing a staff of nursing nuns and a fine chapel.

All this was enough to start me on one of the most complicated watercolor drawings I

The Pagoda of Huang-shan, Hankow, China, 1954. *A wooded height seemed a natural setting for this graceful pagoda. Drawn on Chinese bamboo paper with soft and medium Hardtmuth charcoal leads. From* Looking at China, *1955. Courtesy Lawrence and Wishart, London. Reproduced by permission of the owner, the estate of the late Sir Allen Lane.*

have made. It took me all of three hours to complete in the middle of a freezing November day.

SUITING MEDIUM TO SUBJECT

Christian architecture reaches into my subconscious in a way which not only helps me choose a subject but also enables me to decide, almost at a glance, what medium to use. In 1963, a *Fortune* assignment took me up the Connecticut River Valley. In towns like Windsor, Connecticut, I found myself recalling my own nonconformist religious background. This led me to stop and draw the seventeenth-century Windsor Congregational Church.

It seemed a natural decision to use ink with a Spencerian school nib for the broad lines. I used a Gillot 303 nib for the fine lines; this nib enabled me to define the church's classical style more precisely. For greater emphasis, I used a Japanese brush to fill in the solid areas, such as the roof. Then I added several gravestones to embellish the foreground and illustrate the predominantly English ancestry of the community.

MOSQUES, TEMPLES, AND PAGODAS

Christianity's nearest rival was Islam; yet the mosques of the Arab world, as well as the temples or pagodas of the Far East, create a different set of associations for me. Hence I make different decisions on how to draw them. Mohammedans were sustained in their military ardor by the sensual belief that death in battle against Christian infidels meant an eternity of bliss in a heavenly harem. Thus, at least in my own mind, mosques create an ambiance of a much less demanding and worldly faith than Christianity.

Pagodas, too, have similar associations for me. I find it easier to relate their dazzling opulence to *nirvana* (the extinction of individual existence) rather than to the central belief of most Eastern religions that the principal cause of suffering is desire; the suppression of desire, and consequently of suffering, can only be brought about by discipline. Therefore, my drawings of mosques and pagodas have tended to be much more stylized; they are much more lushly decorative with the em-

phasis placed on color and textural qualities, rather than on more personal associations.

Whatever kind of associations, or feelings, ecclesiastical architecture evokes gives way to them. Let them rise to the surface of your consciousness. Note down these associations just as soon as you have them. In fact, they should act as a main factor when you are deciding which building to draw. If you give free rein to your feelings and associations, the chances are that you will be able not only to draw but to interpret this form of architecture as well.

The Pokrovsky Convent, Suzdal, U.S.S.R., 1967. *Even before I had heard the details of its lurid past, the starkly brooding nature of the place strongly influenced me. I found myself massing the towers and galleries, the eye-like windows, and even including such symbols of death as hovering carrion crows. Drawn on a double sheet of Glastonbury Antique drawing paper with Higgins India ink, a Faber 702 sketching pencil, Faber Markettes, and Grumbacher watercolors. I used a Spencerian school nib and Nos. 4 and 6 Winsor & Newton sable brushes. From* A Russian Journey: from Suzdal to Samarkand, *1969. Courtesy Cassell and Company, London; and Hill & Wang, Inc., New York.*

10
Victorian Architecture

In a changing world, Victorian buildings have long since become obsolete. They constitute a begrimed legacy of rundown city halls, colleges, theaters, railway stations, public markets, department stores, cemeteries, apartments, and private homes. We often do not even bother to look at them twice. Yet not to do so is to lack imagination. Victorian architecture is the richest hunting ground for far-out material.

THREE STAGES OF VICTORIAN ARCHITECTURE

Victorian architecture is incredibly varied, comprising as it does a huge backlog of historical style. To produce this style, architects plundered every period of architecture known to man. Sir Hugh Casson in his admirable survey, *Victorian Architecture* (London, 1948), states that there are three definite epochs. Although he is referring to Victorian architecture in Britain, the same periods generally apply to Victorian buildings in the United States and Canada. The first, or *Romantic* (1832–45), is defined as the tail-end of the eighteenth century. For example, the classical tradition of the Grand Manner in the United States (the Federal style) was then still strong, but was increasingly challenged by an up and coming Gothic revival. In Britain, the period was dominated by Augustus Welby Pugin, the architect of the Houses of Parliament.

The second, or *Christian,* epoch (1845–1860), Casson continues, "has a strong odor of ecclesiology (church-building and decoration)." It is a period of increasing prosperity; this is reflected by the increased use of ornamentation. Its prophet is the art critic John Ruskin (1819-1900) who decreed that the Gothic style was not only for churches, but "could do anything." But he became appalled when he was taken too literally. "There is scarcely a public-house (bar)," he wrote in 1862, "that does not sell its gin and bitters under pseudo-Venetian

Victorian House in the Calle de Teniente Mulet Garcia, Palma, Majorca, 1964. *(Right) I repeatedly find myself drawing houses I would like to live in. Like this one with stone, cigar-store type Indian figures standing side by side with classical maidens. Drawn with 3B, 5B, and 7B Venus graphite pencils on Saunders paper. From* Majorca Observed, *1965. Courtesy Cassell and Company, London; and Doubleday & Company, Inc., New York.*

Paul Hogarth

PALMA: EL TERRENO
House in Pl. Calle del
Teniente Mulet GARCIA

Victorian Warehouses, Front and Chestnut Streets, Philadelphia, 1968. *I selected this one out of a whole block and drew it with a combination of Faber Markers, Grumbacher watercolors, and Higgins India ink—for line and as a wash. The passing figure was caught with a Faber 702 sketching pencil. From "Hogarth's Philadelphia," Philadelphia Inquirer, March 9, 1969. Reproduced by permission of the owner, David Felder, Trenton, New Jersey.*

capitals." He also turned on those who dared to apply his doctrine to industrial buildings. You could not count on pleasing Ruskin.

The third, or *Secular,* epoch (1860–1895), known also as High Victorian (no pun intended), is even more flamboyantly ornate. During the last phase of Queen Victoria's life, the style expressed stuffy gentility, or so it seems to us today. However, this period of time was a robust, uninhibited era of unlimited wealth. In North America, this period reached its climax in luxurious and staggeringly costly residential "palaces" built by the millionaires of New York and Chicago. Cornelius Vanderbilt spent four million dollars building a seventy-room summer home at Newport, Rhode Island; it had bathrooms fitted with hot and cold running salt water in addition to the regular kind. The megalomaniacal taste of the railroad barons was also responsible for a chain of huge florid hotels (built mostly by the Northern Pacific and the Canadian Pacific Railways) set amidst the majestic peaks of the Rockies. Even if High Victorian comprised all of Victorian architecture, it would be more than enough to make it my favorite!

VICTORIAN ARCHITECTURE IN AMERICA

I particularly relish the Victorian architect's sense of manifest opulence. You can imagine my feelings when I turned a corner in Banff, Alberta, Canada during the summer of 1969 and found myself face to face with the Canadian Pacific's fabulous Banff Springs Hotel. Built in 1887 at the juncture of the Bow and Spray rivers, this place really is "High" Victorian! Its style, a giant-sized amalgam of Chateau Gothic and Scots Baronial, makes you wonder if that really was Boris Karloff you saw behind the reception desk.

In a slightly higher bracket of ingenuity are the buildings of the Pennsylvania Academy of the Fine Arts, and the Old Penn Library of the University of Pennsylvania. Both were designed by Frank Furness, Philadelphia's contributor to Victorian architecture. I never was able to finish my watercolor drawing of the Academy building. The winter drove me inside the building to brood in frustration. But I was more fortunate with the Old Penn Library, which I depicted

(continued on page 105)

Chinatown, Philadephia, 1968. *I combined pencil with markers and watercolor for this vignette of China in America. Distinctly ethnic neighborhoods, such as this one, provide an exciting way to depict the exotic, all encompassing flavor of a city. The figures were drawn in with a Spencerian school nib and Pelikan Fount India ink in an 11″ x 14″ sketchbook of three-ply, high surface Strathmore drawing paper. An un-published drawing from my stay in Pennsylvania.*

The Rooftops of Beaune, France, 1970. *(Above) Joyfully expecting good things, I arrived in the celebrated Burgundian wine capital for the traditional wine-tasting festivities known as* Les Trois Glorieuses *(Three Glorious Days). I drew this in about one and a half hours with a Faber 702 sketching pencil and Faber Design Markettes. I used a custom-made 15" x 20" sketchbook of Glastonbury Antique drawing paper. I applied washes of Winsor & Newton and Grumbacher watercolors with a Japanese brush and a No. 3 sable later when I was back in my hotel room. From "Three Glorious Days of Burgundian Bacchanalia" for the* Daily Telegraph Magazine, *London, September 17, 1971. Reproduced by permission of the owners, Mr. and Mrs. Kenneth Twist, Cambridge, England.*

Eton College, England, 1968. *(Right) Founded in 1440 by Henry the Sixth, the older buildings at Eton are almost entirely Tudor in style. This bird's-eye view shows the school yard with its statue of King Henry; Lupton's Tower stands at the top. I worked from three viewpoints and used a combination of pen, pencil, ink line and wash, and watercolor. I used a Venus 7B graphite pencil, Spencerian and Gillot 303 nibs, Pelikan Fount India ink and Grumbacher watercolors. My drawing surface was Daler drawing paper. From a portfolio on Eton for* Boys' Life *magazine, November, 1971. Courtesy Boys' Life magazine, New York.*

Paul HOGARTH : Moscow

Cathedral of St. Basil, Red Square, Moscow, U.S.S.R., 1967. (Left) *Multicolored and multidomed, St. Basil's is a fairy-like structure in paint and stone. It was built by Ivan the Terrible to commemorate his historic victory over the Tartar hordes. It is said that the capricious Tsar summoned the two luckless architects—Barma and Posnik—and, after congratulations, ordered that their eyes be put out so that they might never again design anything so enchantingly beautiful. I painted this with Winsor & Newton watercolors and Faber Markettes over a graphite pencil outline. From A Russian Journey: from Suzdal to Samarkand, 1969. Courtesy Cassell and Company, London; and Hill & Wang, Inc., New York.*

United Nations Building, East River, New York, 1968. (Above) *On the island of Manhattan, skyscrapers push and jostle each other like pine trees in a forest. It is a sight brimful of new energy. With such a cityscape—just like a landscape—selection is important in order to draw it well. I used three-ply, medium surface Strathmore illustration board. Winsor & Newton watercolors, Faber Markettes, Nos. 1, 5 and 9 Winsor & Newton sable brushes, and a Faber 702 sketching pencil were my drawing media. Originally reproduced in color as a greeting card. Courtesy American Artists Group, New York.*

Art Nouveau Apartment House, Moscow, 1967. *Moscow is a gold mine of exotic architecture; of all the world's capital cities, it alone has the greatest variety of styles. This ship-like Art Nouveau apartment block in the Arbat quarter, designed by Shekhtel, was a delight to draw. Before the revolution it provided spacious studios for painters; it is now a tenement. I did this drawing in about an hour and a half in a custom-made 15″ x 20″ sketchbook of Glastonbury Antique drawing paper. I used a Faber 702 sketching pencil and Winsor & Newton watercolors. From* A Russian Journey: from Suzdal to Samarkand, *1969. Courtesy Cassell and Company, London; and Hill & Wang, Inc., New York.*

Grauman's Chinese Theater, Hollywood, 1971. *In that fabulous frenzied suburb of Los Angeles, called Hollywood, you are apt to find a bit of everything, whether you may be looking for it or not. I found Grauman's Chinese on Hollywood Boulevard; I stayed there for every minute of three hours, reveling in its oriental "showbiz" ambiance, complete with the hand, leg, and footprints of the stars! I did this drawing in a custom-made, 15" x 20" sketchbook of Glastonbury Antique drawing paper, especially bound so I could draw across two pages. I used a Faber 702 sketching pencil, Faber Design Markettes, and washes of Winsor & Newton Artists Quality watercolors applied with a Japanese brush. The figures were drawn with a Gillot 303 nib and Higgins India ink. Reproduced by permission of the owner, Richard Gangel, Greenwich, Connecticut.*

High River, Alberta, Canada, 1969. *Indian raids, gun-totin' cowboys, ranches with great herds of cattle and horses, log cabins, land-hungry homesteaders, grain, oil, and an internationally famous polo team are all part of the historic background of High River. With its wild oats scattered long ago, the town has settled down to a peaceful life on the vast plains of Southern Alberta. I completed the drawing in some two hours using a Faber 702 sketching pencil, Faber Markettes, Winsor & Newton water-colors, a Japanese brush and a No. 5 Winsor & Newton sable brush. Reproduced by permission of the owner, Graham Greene, Switzerland.*

(continued from page 96)

earlier in the fall when the weather was still fine. In fact, it furnished such good material that it is well worth describing how I made the drawing.

CAPTURING THE VICTORIAN SPIRIT

For once, I did not even stop to make my customary composition sketch. I immediately set to work making a light pencil outline with a 3B pencil. Then I used a Faber 702 pencil to develop the drawing. But I soon switched to color to capture the building's peculiar spooky ambiance. I filled in the entire pencil outline with a pink Faber Design Markette as the first stage of rendering the building's sugary, reddish-pink sandstone, faintly discernible under a film of grime.

Then something made me pause and feel more than ever that this was going to be a good drawing. Very few students entered the library. Among those who did, there was more than one white-faced, long-haired girl in an ankle-length gown. I responded to my subject with renewed interest! I restrained myself from adding these flying figures on broomsticks! Nevertheless, the message was clear. This was no ordinary library.

Quickly, I penciled in two or three of these girls in a pocket-sized sketchbook so that I could add them to my drawing later. While doing so, I noticed a gaunt, bare tree in the right foreground. Another prop to build upon! I drew it in soft pencil; then I proceeded to define in black India ink the rows of mullioned, eye-like windows and water spouts fashioned in the shape of grotesque animal faces. Finally, I laid in diluted ink washes to simulate the Library's accumulated grime.

Allow the eccentricities of Victorian architecture to engage and spark your imagination. Whether you employ humor or caricature is up to you. Your response, of course, may not *always* be appropriate. Being able to view such richly visual architecture with a free-wheeling sense of fun is the key to a successful and personal interpretation of it. This personal response, or interpretation, is, after all, as much a part of drawing as are your marks on paper.

City Meat and Fish Market, Kiev, U.S.S.R., 1967. *Oddly shaped turn-of-the-century buildings are often easy to draw because of their visually eccentric character. I used graphite pencil with washes of diluted Higgins India ink and touches of Winsor & Newton watercolor. Drawn in a 15" x 20" sketchbook of Glastonbury Antique drawing paper. From A Russian Journey: from Suzdal to Samarkand, 1969. Courtesy Cassell and Company, London; and Hill & Wang, Inc., New York.*

Dun Laoghaire, Ireland, 1964–1969. *In this pleasant resort a few miles out of Dublin, you can go right back to Victorian times. Gothic villas line the seafront and there are tea-shops with displays of cakes straight out of Mrs. Beeton's celebrated cookbook. Drawn with a Faber 702 sketching pencil and washes of Higgins India ink in an 11" x 14" sketchbook of Strathmore drawing paper. Reprinted from Lithopinion 16. © 1969 by Local One, Amalgamated Lithographers of America, New York.*

Victorian Fountain, Dun Laoghaire, Ireland, 1964–1969. *Across from the villas pictured on the opposite page, there is even a fountain erected to commemorate Queen Victoria's Diamond Jubilee in 1897. Drawn with 5B and 7B Venus graphite pencils on Saunders paper. Courtesy the Shelbourne Hotel, Dublin, Ireland.*

Leningrad: Alexander Nevsky
Monastery, Necropolis of
the distinguished writers
musicians and artists of the
nineteenth century.

VICTORIAN CEMETERIES

Also characteristic of the Victorian period are huge cemeteries crowned with ornate tombstones and mausoleums. The craving of wealthy Victorians to establish themselves after death in what they believed to be baronial splendor is found throughout Europe and the United States. Highgate and Kensal Green, London; Glasnevin, Dublin; Père Lachaise, Paris; and Bay Ridge, Brooklyn are among the most outstanding Victorian cemeteries from the architectural point of view. But the old municipal cemeteries of Glasgow, Genoa, and Vienna run closely behind.

However, the most impressive of all these cemeteries is the *Literatorskiye Mostki*, or Literary Necropolis, of the Volkov Cemetery on the grounds of the Alexander Nevsky Cathedral, Leningrad; this is the national and eternal resting-place for celebrated men-of-letters, scientists, musicians, and artists. Here, scattered in splendid profusion are huge marble and stone memorials, urns, obelisks, and mausoleums housing the remains of the writers Turgenev, Blok, and Dostoevsky; the physicist Pavlov; the composers Scriabin and Rimsky-Korsakov; the pianist Rubenstein; and the painter Isaac Brodsky. Stylistically these monuments are extraordinary examples of Victorian architectural necrophilia. I would add that Bay Ridge, Brooklyn runs a close second with its far-out monument to the Brooklyn dead of the Civil War as well as a giant-sized stone baseball on the tomb of the Englishman who devised the game's rules. In Leningrad, the life-size, stone streetcar on top of the tomb of its inventor is also worthy of mention.

The Victorian custom of visiting the graves of beloved relatives is still widespread in Ireland and in Spain. Take care to observe an attitude of respect, otherwise drawing in cemeteries (especially those in Catholic European countries) might involve you with someone's outraged piety.

One day, in 1963, I was happily drawing a fine Art Nouveau tomb in the Palma Municipal Cemetery with not a soul in sight. Suddenly, an angry protest broke about my head. A stout old lady had spotted me and was telling me off for being disrespectful to the dead. I managed to calm her by saying no disrespect was implied and left; I returned later, when the coast was clear, to complete the drawing.

An experience I had in a Leningrad cemetery in 1967 was the opposite. I had made a drawing in black graphite pencil of the *Literatorskiye Mostki* mentioned earlier and was about to leave through the cemetery's tiny entrance porch. The weather was bitterly cold, but my heavy winter outfit made me too warm. I paused outside to take off my cap to mop a fevered brow with a Kleenex. Being the Easter season, it was an old Russian custom to be charitable at that time of year. So thinking that I needed alms, a little old *babushka,* or peasant woman, tossed five kopecks (ten cents) into my cap!

Seriously, take a good look at your local cemetery. Victorian or Edwardian, they usually offer a wide variety of ornament and style. And, in spite of the above experiences, you can usually count on drawing them in peace.

The Literary Necropolis, Volkov Cemetery, Leningrad, 1967. *In the middle of the nineteenth century, the Volkov Cemetery became a national pantheon —the last resting place of Russia's most illustrious intellectuals. Overwhelmed by the sepulchral eeriness and the biting cold of Leningrad in April, I was only able to include (from left to right), the painter Brodsky, the writer Dostoevski, the composer Scriabin, and the pianist Rubinstein (bust only). Nevertheless, their flamboyant, Slavic-Victorian, brown and black marble gravestones were a joy to draw. Drawn entirely with a Faber 702 sketching pencil in a 15″ x 20″ sketchbook of Glastonbury Antique paper. From* A Russian Journey: from Suzdal to Samarkand, *1969. Courtesy Cassell and Co. London; Hill & Wang, Inc., New York.*

11
Art Nouveau Architecture

As the nineteenth century drew to an end, groups of young artists, architects, and designers withdrew to the country to think out their protest against the pomposities and vulgarities of the Victorian era. New magazines appeared: *The Studio* (London, 1893); *Jugend* (Munich, 1896); *Vers Sacrum* (Vienna, 1897) and *Mir Isskustva* (St. Petersburg, 1898). These magazines helped launch a new style—one that was as sinuous as the unfolding organism of a young fern shoot.

Architecture shook off the look of ornate respectability. Roofs were swept and bent with snakelike abandon. Windows were made to bulge like leaf-shaped eyes set in blue-green beds of ceramic tile. Wrought-iron was made to assume the guise of tortuous exotic flowers and twisted plants. The new style spread like a fever under a variety of labels: it was Art Nouveau in England and America; *Le Style Moderne* in France; *Jugendstil* in Germany; *Sezession* in Austria; *Stile Liberty* in Italy; and *Modernista* in Spain. Wherever the movement manifested itself, it set out to revolutionize architecture, interior design, and household objects. Music, painting, sculpture, and book and magazine illustration all played their part in influencing and, in turn, beng influenced by Art Nouveau.

ART NOUVEAU IN EUROPE AND AMERICA

Perhaps the most strikingly visual examples of the style are found in Barcelona; the nightmarish and wildly Gothic extravangaza of the Church Sagrada Familia, and the extraordinary apartment houses, Casa Batillo and Casa Mila. They are the work of Antonio Gaudí (1852–1926) but look as though they might have been

Dom Gorodetskogo, Kiev, U.S.S.R., 1967. *(Right) This unusual mansion was designed and built by a merchant named Gorodetski, who was also an engineer and an architect. The house was approaching completion in 1912 when he received the tragic news that his much loved and only daughter had gone down with the Titanic. He, thereupon, commissioned the elaborate sculptured frieze containing art nouveau maidens cavorting with amiable monsters of the deep. Drawn with a Faber 702 sketching pencil and washes of Higgins India ink. From* A Russian Journey: from Suzdal to Samarkand, *1969. Courtesy Cassell and Company, London; and Hill & Wang, Inc., New York.*

Paul HOGARTH

KIEV: DOM GORODETSKOGO

Yaroslavsky Railway Station, 1967. *(Above) Shekhtel's most fabulous building, however, is this station on Komsomolskaya Square. Built in 1905, it looks more like the beginning of a Russian fairy tale than a railway starting point to Yaroslav, or indeed anywhere. Also drawn with a Faber 702 sketching pencil on Glastonbury Antique paper. From A Russian Journey: from Suzdal to Samarkand, 1969. Courtesy Cassell and Company, London; and Hill & Wang, Inc., New York. Reproduced by permission of the owner, Peter Scott, London, England.*

Ryabouchinsky House, 1967. *(Right) Another Shekhtel design is the exquisite, yellow former home of the famous ballerina Ryabouchinskaya in Verousky Street, Arbat. After the revolution, the writer Maxim Gorki lived there from 1931 to 1936. Drawn with a Faber 702 sketching pencil and washes of Grumbacher watercolor in a 15" x 20" sketchbook of Glastonbury Antique paper. Courtesy Cassell and Company, London; and Hill & Wang, Inc., New York. Reproduced by permission of the owner, Anthony Bell, London, England.*

Paul Stevenson Oles
Moscow. Ryzbdschinsky House

Paul Hogarth. Moscow Art Theatre

designed by Vincent Price, Edgar Allen Poe, Boris Karloff, and partners. Other Art Nouveau buildings designed by no less talented architects are to be found throughout Europe and in America.

For example, Brussels has Victor Horta's masterpiece, a splendid house at 6 rue Paul Emile Janson; Chicago still has a few buildings by Louis Sullivan, although (sadly) some sixty-six of his pioneer structures have been demolished. Glasgow has the superb School of Art designed by Charles Rennie Mackintosh. Moscow, a city which usually gets left out of the studies and monographs devoted to the period, has a rich crop of ornate houses, ship-like apartment blocks, the Moscow Art Theater, and a railroad station straight out of a fairy tale; most are the work of F. O. Shekhtel. Paris, of course, has the celebrated cast iron Métro entrances designed by Hector Guimard. Because it was a style patronized by enlightened entrepreneurs of the time, many buildings are also to be found in provincial cities with a commercial tradition, such as Buffalo in the United States, Manchester and Liverpool in England, Kiev in the U.S.S.R., Lyons in France, and Amsterdam in Holland.

A VANISHING STYLE

Never put off drawing an Art Nouveau building. Although the new style flowered for some thirty years, architectural examples are fast dwindling. An Art Nouveau building is rarely given a reprieve once it is slated for demolition. As I write, particularly in Spain, many examples of this architecture are being torn down. Many more have already been replaced by featureless and undistinguished modern blocks. In both Europe and North America, few authorities realize or have been made to realize the artistic importance of these buildings and have refused to save them from developers who seek to replace them with more profitable office buildings or parking garages.

CREATIVE EXPRESSION AND ART NOUVEAU

Art Nouveau is, by far, the most delightful of all architectural styles to draw. I think this is because it offers such a welcome release from the disciplines necessary to capture the essence of most other styles. Art Nouveau buildings are so richly inventive in their fantasy that I gaze at them with fascination. Therefore, to draw them is, indeed, an unexpected pleasure.

Usually, their bubbling complexity forces me to think in terms of buoyantly massive shapes. Sometimes I feel as if I have a huge piece of modeling clay in my hands instead of a pencil. I begin with an outline, as I always do. But very soon I feel compelled to start with color; I apply it broadly, using watercolor or markers as my medium. Then, I get back to drawing again, freely developing the curving, rising forms with a 3B pencil. Finally, I revert to color, working with a No. 0 or No. 1 sable brush to pick out what I feel to be the most exciting, visually significant details of the building.

Drawing Art Nouveau offers a departure point for seeing architecture in a much more totally visual way. It may do more. I know it has enabled me to go on and explore as well as to appreciate the nuances of more eclectic styles such as 1920's "Constructivism" and 1930's "Aztec." If traditional styles prevent you from thinking of architecture as living, colorful subject matter, Art Nouveau might well help remove that block.

The Moscow Art Theater, 1967. *The Russians seem left out of the Art Nouveau league. Yet, as this and the following drawing show, they have equally fascinating examples of an architectural idiom that synthesizes Celtic, Greek, Japanese, Byzantine, and now Slavic strains. Designed by F. O. Shekhtel in 1904, this theater sports a voluptuous bas-relief by the painter M. A. Vrubel. Drawn with a Faber 702 sketching pencil, Grumbacher watercolors and diluted Higgins India ink. From* A Russian Journey: from Suzdal to Samarkand, *1969. Courtesy Cassell and Company, London; and Hill & Wang, Inc., New York.*

12
Industrial Architecture

Industrial architecture and engineering projects offer the artist a uniquely different challenge. In older industrial regions, like England's grim northwest, for example, an occasional confrontation with the poignantly faded beauty of a Victorian Lancashire cotton mill is no less pictorially dramatic than the sight of a huge new dam. I think of one such dam that I saw being constructed in a mountain valley of relatively undeveloped Yugoslavia; that dam will transform the living standards in that country. Drawing industrial architecture, whether it is old or new, is more than just drawing a building: such drawing can embody the substance of the artist's response to his time.

THE INDUSTRIAL SCENE

Artists have been fascinated and repelled by industrialization since its early days. Almost immediately, industrial subjects entered the art of topographical artists; they made an almost complete record of the marvels of what they felt to be a new era. Coal pits in remote landscapes, mills on the banks of idyllic rivers, and above all ironworks with blazing furnaces and noisy forges appealed to the connoisseurs of the picturesque as perfect examples of the sublime. Great works of industrial architecture were accorded the status of classical antiquities and often depicted as picturesque ruins.

A sense of discovery was characteristic of the luminous and delicate vigor of the industrial "views" of Paul Sandby (1725–1809). Phillip James de Loutherbourg (1740–1812), J. M. W. Turner (1778–1851), John Sell Cotman (1782–1842), and other English watercolorists recorded their impressions right down to the colored drawings made by great architect-engineers like Thomas Telford (1757–1834). All these artists displayed in their works infectious romanticism and faith in progress. By the mid-nineteenth century, however, this sentiment had shifted in the opposite direction. Artists, in general, came to abhor the industrial "view" and expressed their despair at the pollution and abject poverty which always seemed to be the price of industrial growth. A sense of the sublime is totally absent from Gustave Doré's nightmarish industrial buildings drawn for his immense album, *London: a Pilgrimage* (London, 1871).

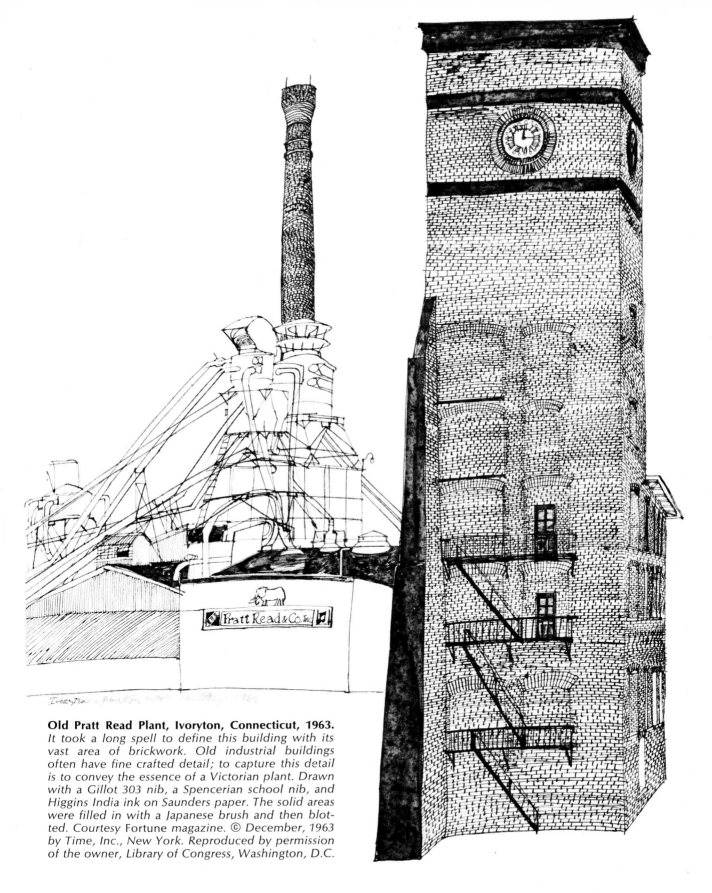

Old Pratt Read Plant, Ivoryton, Connecticut, 1963.
It took a long spell to define this building with its vast area of brickwork. Old industrial buildings often have fine crafted detail; to capture this detail is to convey the essence of a Victorian plant. Drawn with a Gillot 303 nib, a Spencerian school nib, and Higgins India ink on Saunders paper. The solid areas were filled in with a Japanese brush and then blotted. Courtesy Fortune magazine. © December, 1963 by Time, Inc., New York. Reproduced by permission of the owner, Library of Congress, Washington, D.C.

UHOBARA
Tanjica Power Project
Lovac

INDUSTRY AND TODAY'S ARTIST

Artists today look at the industrial scene with the same uneasy consciences. Socially oriented artists like Edward Hopper, Reginald Marsh, Ben Shahn, Daniel Scharz, Robert Andrew Parker and Robert Weaver have used industrial architecture as a subject for creative interpretation. For them (and for me also), Time Inc.'s *Fortune* provided the space for such illustrations. The magazine has enabled artists to travel throughout America, and the world at large, to depict the construction or the existence of great industrial projects and buildings. For the first time since the nineteenth century, *Fortune* encouraged the artist to step out of his studio.

The work of those artists, therefore, and of many others is well worth looking at. You will find their industrial portfolios in the bound volumes of *Fortune* from 1930 to the present day which you may (if you are lucky) find in your city library. If not, check the *American Union List of Serials* or *British Union Catalogue of Periodicals*. You may find a set in some specialist or university library in your district or nearby city.

PLACES TO GO

You will never be without material if you live in the United States or in Britain. Those who live in or near big industrial cities—such as Chicago, Montreal, Pittsburgh, and New York or Birmingham, Glasgow, Liverpool, Leeds or Manchester—will have the widest selection of buildings to choose from. But even the smallest town or city will have its share, if not of old plants and factories, then certainly new ones with their sometimes "science fiction" exteriors.

Besides factory buildings of every period, there are also workshops, mills, warehouses,

---

The Trebisnijica Dam, Yugoslavia, 1967. *Strictly speaking, dams, like bridges, are engineering projects but I like to think of them as being halfway to architecture and certainly they can be drawn as such. I used an X-shaped composition for this giant dam under construction in southeast Herzegovina. I wanted above all to convey its monumental scale and sense of power. Drawn with a Faber 702 sketching pencil in a 14" x 17" sketchbook of Strathmore Alexis drawing paper. Courtesy* Fortune *magazine. © May, 1967 by Time, Inc., New York.*

and bridges (discussed separately in Chapter 13). Sharpen your powers of observation and increase your knowledge by trying to determine when these structures were built. Much industrial architecture, until quite recently, was derived from the changes in our architectural taste. These "fashionable" architectural styles were sometimes utilized on amusingly and grandiose scale. For example, such styles as 1930's "Aztec" factories and warehouses make an ideal theme for a whole series of industrial drawings.

You may find, as I did, that if a particular period fascinates you it is often a short cut to not only a deeper appreciation of architecture generally, but to the finer points of drawing it as well.

HOW TO DRAW INDUSTRIAL SUBJECTS

Many of the problems I have discussed in regard to drawing historical or vernacular architecture can also be applied to drawing industrial subjects. How I draw a factory also depends on both the time I have available and on the pictorial interest the shape or structure may possess. Moreover, a factory, like other architectural subjects, can look very different at various times of the day; an oil refinery, for example, might be better depicted at night rather than by day. The multicolored flames belching from tall, chimney-like retorts contrasted against the night sky increase the refinery's pictorial interest. On the other hand, daylight might be more appropriate for the study of a Palladian-classical type 1920's automobile plant whose stylistic eccentricities will require totally different lighting conditions.

Drawing the exterior of an industrial building may involve you in much the same bustle and confusion as you will find on a city street. Therefore, it is advisable to use similar approaches and procedures when making such drawings. My notebook habit is a particularly helpful aid which enables me to make a general analysis of a building. This analysis, or digest of my subject, is the first step towards producing an effective composition.

Usually, I avoid too literal a perspective system, unless it can be put to good dramatic advantage. Instead, I rely on creating a flat or foreshortened composition which permits me

MOSTAR, Paul Hogarth

to develop the inherent shape of the building or installation. Then I can exploit any textural qualities the building may have. I will also use whatever accessories may be available to increase the visual impact of my drawing. For example, an elevated expressway or railroad track might make an effective counterpoint to, say, an old industrial plant.

DRAWING MEDIA

You will find that different styles of industrial subjects suggest different media. The "science-fiction" look of many new industrial plants might call for a bubbly delicacy combined with bright vivid colors; in this case, watercolor over pencil, or colored inks over pen may be the right choices. On the other hand, older, more brutal-looking subjects that involve vast areas of open brickwork, graced with billboards, and slashed with power lines may defy interpretation in such media. Such subjects make me feel equally anarchic and tempt me to make drawings with a fat brush loaded with ink. I may even confine myself to pens and drawing ink to provide the textural range and contrast necessary to interpret this kind of subject.

Texture is particularly important. In the absence of the finesse of the Grand Manner style, I have to exploit what is visually available in order to give my drawing punch and tension. In this way, I can match the stark monumental character of the massive, brooding industrialism of yesteryear.

There are times when I will draw a sleazy old factory for no other reason than moral indignation—just because this was a place where some one actually *had* to work fourteen hours a day. This is another vital clue to seeing industrial architecture in a much more imaginative way.

Mostar, Yugoslavia, 1967. *My object in making this composite pencil and wash drawing was to depict the advent of industrialization in this sleepy Bosnian town. Mostar was ruled by the Turks from 1566 to 1875; the famous bridge (upper right) was built in 1566. But Mostar is quickly acquiring a modern look with bauxite plants, cotton mills, and an aircraft factory. Drawn with a Faber 702 sketching pencil and washes of Higgins India ink in a 14" x 17" sketchbook of Strathmore Alexis drawing paper. Courtesy* Fortune *magazine. © May, 1967 by Time, Inc., New York.*

Try to imagine how it must have felt to have worked in, say, a New Jersey textile mill a hundred years ago, or even today. Alternatively, you might provide yourself with an exercise, such as the following that I gave to a group of my students at the Royal College of Art.

SOCIAL ISSUES

The exercise was none other than that shockingly neglected issue which environmentalists have long campaigned about—pollution. Each student had to search for the possibilities in a given industrial area and develop them as he wished. Forbidding-looking industrial buildings or installations, if seen as ominous shapes, could be equated with the production of poisonous wastes which are such a hazard to wildlife and human health.

Industrial architecture—such as paper mills, fertilizer factories, and chemical plants—became a point of departure for a series of freewheeling graphic indictments. These drawings exploited to the fullest extent the inherent eccentricities of these structures. My students had a vast amount of subjects to choose from in the industrial East End of London, but there is no reason why you should not investigate less spectacular cases in your own area. My students discovered that the exercise not only tapped their sense of personal initiative (they were given two weeks to find and depict a subject), but their social consciences as well. Moreover, they were able to use the exercise to develop a visual awareness of industrial buildings in relation to drawing architecture. In this way, their ability to draw was related to a subject they had seldom, if ever, tackled. If you are stumped or stalled by industrial architecture, try this exercise sometime.

13
Bridges

Anyone who has seen a fine looking bridge silhouetted against the dying light of a summer day is not likely to forget the sight. Bridges symbolize the determination of man to shape a hostile environment to his needs. Even in the most grimly uncompromising urban or industrial settings, their essentially functional character often provides a dynamic and awe-inspiringly beautiful spectacle.

CHOOSING YOUR MEDIUM

Unless their essential structures are carefully observed, bridges are not easy to draw. If you are alert and get the fundamentals right, the rest is largely a matter of finding the most appropriate medium to use. I usually think of bridges as black and white subjects. Arch bridges of stone, for example, particularly lend themselves to freely detailed definition with a soft graphite pencil, a charcoal lead, charcoal pencils, carbon pencils, and Conté and Hardtmuth crayons.

On the other hand, iron bridges of every type invite more adventuresome combinations of ink, pencil, and wash. To draw such bridges I sometimes use a large watercolor brush, like a No. 9 Winsor & Newton; I charge it fully with India ink and work it over a light pencil outline, blotting to emphasize the rich textural effects of the cast iron work.

ARCH BRIDGES

A bridge consists of two supports, one at each end, called *abutments;* a *span* connects these two abutments. The intermediate supports are called *piers.* There are four main types of bridges: arch, girder, suspension, and movable.

Arch bridges of stone or brick are the earliest extant. Their form may be semicircular (as in Roman viaducts) or elliptical. Pointed or Gothic arches, like the hump-backed, or "devil's bridge," are also encountered in isolated villages throughout Europe and Asia, and oddly enough over canals in the older industrial regions of England, such as Lancashire. Modern metal arch bridges are usually built of steel lattice, such as the one at Niagara Falls, New York. One of the largest metal arch bridges is the Sydney Harbor Bridge, Australia, built in 1932. Arch bridges can also be made of con-

Tower Bridge

Tower Bridge, London, 1966. *I saw this Gothic, Victorian bascule bridge as a hardworking edifice. So I got up and drew it in the early morning to catch the surging flow of traffic crossing into central London. Drawn in an 11" x 14" sketchbook of Strathmore Alexis drawing paper with a Faber 702 graphite sketching pencil. From London à la Mode, 1966. Courtesy Studio Vista, Ltd., London; and Hill & Wang, Inc., New York. Reproduced by permission of the owner, Gillian Greenwood, London, England.*

Albert Bridge,
Chelsea

crete, like the present Waterloo bridge, London, built in 1945.

GIRDER BRIDGES

Each span of a girder bridge consists of two or more iron girders laid parallel and connected by cross-pieces and plates, a vertical web, and a bottom plate parallel to the top one; the Tay bridge of 1887 in Scotland is a classic example of this type of bridge. The great trestle bridges which carried the first transcontinental railroads across the deep canyons of the Old West were built of timber.

For greater spans, the cantilever system is used; a famous example of such a bridge is the Forth Railway Bridge of 1890 in Scotland. Another is the Quebec Bridge in Canada, built in 1917; it has a central span of 1,800 feet.

SUSPENSION BRIDGES

Of course, the best of all bridges to draw are suspension bridges. Their delicate webs of wire cables give them an air of balanced elegance. These cables consist of several hundred separate strands passed over the tops of tall steel or stone towers and anchored to the ground behind the towers.

One of the first notable examples is the suspension bridge built at Clifton, near Bristol, England; it was designed by I. K. Brunel in 1864. The Borough of Manhattan in New York City also has several fine Victorian specimens of suspension bridges, but these are dwarfed by such modern examples as the Golden Gate suspension bridge, San Francisco, and the Verrazano-Narrows double-deckered bridge between Brooklyn and Staten Island, New York.

MOVABLE BRIDGES

Finally, there are the movable types. These comprise low bridges across rivers, canals, or

Albert Bridge, Chelsea, London, 1966. *The almost oriental grace of suspension bridges makes the task of drawing riverscapes both easy and delightful. Drawn with a Faber 702 sketching pencil on a 20" x 25" sheet of Strathmore medium surface drawing paper. From* London à la Mode, 1966. *Courtesy Studio Vista, Ltd., London; and Hill & Wang, Inc., New York.*

The Halfpenny Bridge, Dublin, 1964. *This structure is so named because in the old days a halfpenny was the toll charge for crossing the Liffey River at this point. Bridge crossings are good places to observe not only buildings but people. Drawn on Strathmore charcoal paper with 5B and 6B Venus graphite pencils. Courtesy the Shelbourne Hotel, Dublin, Ireland.*

harbors with movable sections to permit the passage of ships. Four kinds of movable bridges predominate: the *bascule,* the *swing bridge,* the *rolling bridge,* and the *transporter bridge.* The Tower Bridge of 1894 over the Thames in London is an example of the bascule; with this type of movable bridge a roadway section can be raised like a pair of huge trap doors.

In the swing bridge, the roadway pivots at the bridge's center and can be swung around horizontally.

The rolling bridge consists of two parts: one part is fixed but the hollow beneath it contains rows of steel rollers. When the bridge opens, the movable part is telescoped into the fixed part, running beneath it on rollers.

Transporter bridges usually consist of two great towers joined at their tops by a lattice girder, along which a trolley runs on rails. A small platform the width of a road is suspended at road level, and carries vehicles across a river or canal.

LIGHTING AND AMBIANCE

As with most forms of architecture, the time of day you choose to draw a bridge will make an enormous difference. The angle of light causes certain shadow patterns. But more important, the quality of light affects your enthusiasm and, therefore, the quality of your completed drawing. I always find it worthwhile to observe such differences in a notebook before making a final decision. An ordinary looking bridge may take on a totally different personality at night or at sunrise.

Bridges take on a specific character or ambiance from the type of traffic that goes over and underneath them. I remember making what I thought to be a dynamically rendered drawing of Tower Bridge, London, during the summer of 1965. I had placed the bridge in a sharply receding perspective, using a soft graphite pencil that strongly accented this. But there was something lacking. One fussy, self-important tugboat plowing its way underneath activated the entire composition and made all the difference. Be on the lookout for such subsidiary elements whether they are boats, people, or seagulls. All these things can invigorate your drawing by adding local color.

PERSPECTIVE

Bridges can be quite dramatic when drawn with the appropriate perspective system. Let me give you an example. In 1964 I was in Dublin drawing the famous old footbridge known as the Halfpenny Bridge over the Liffey by Bachelor's Walk. It is elegantly arched, cast in iron, and good to draw from almost any position. I decided to draw it head-on in foreshortened perspective to exaggerate its height. In this way I could fill the bridge with a flow of animated figures moving to and from the opposite side. It was also a viewpoint which enabled me to also include a row of fine old Victorian gas lamps—the dramatic touch I was after. Try out different perspective systems before you start your final drawing. It will help you to analyze the character of your subject, and thus enable you to add a dramatic touch.

Whether you draw a part or the whole bridge, be sure to look closely at the juncture at either end where the bridge joins with the opposite side. In most cases, the level of a bridge is continued on the same horizontal plane. Whatever angle, viewpoint, or perspective system you finally use, this horizontal will help you maintain the essential structure of a bridge while enabling you to develop a much more spontaneous drawing.

Finally, I strongly recommend a study of the master Japanese Ukiyo-e printmakers, particularly Hiroshige (1797–1858), for their natural and stylized use of perspective. Hiroshige's famous cycle of prints, *One Hundred Views of Famous Places in Edo* includes many bridge scenes. They show that only half a bridge, or even a single pier, can graphically convey all you need to say about a bridge. Some of these can be seen in the paperback, *Hiroshige,* in the *Masterworks of Ukiyo-e* series (Kodansha International, Tokyo and Palo Alto, California).

14
Architecture and the City

Much of the fascination of the big city emanates from its anarchic aggregation of structures. Viewed with horror by architects and planners, the tumbled chaos of skyscrapers, tenements, expressways, and rundown neighborhoods offers the artist his most dynamic architectural subject—the cityscape.

When I saw New York for the first time in 1962, cityscape entered my artistic repertory with a bang. I viewed with awe the tremendous skyward-thrusting mass of buildings; they jostled each other in a dramatic free-for-all. I felt stunned; the succession of startling sights made me feel like a scrambled jigsaw puzzle. Such a skyline is an architectural symbol of rugged individualism. It expresses, as nothing else does, the vital, energetic, and competitive pulse of American life.

TAKING IT ALL IN

On that first trip to New York I felt I had to immediately translate my feelings into drawings, but I quickly found that a cityscape made new demands. I had to expose myself to the full impact of a big city vista, not so much to be able to draw what I saw, but to build up a personal response to all of it. Therefore, it was vital to find the right vantage point. A Circle Line boat trip, a ride on the elevated subway to Coney Island, and a crossing on the Staten Island Ferry—all were revelations for me. Gradually, I was able to organize my impressions. With the help of a map, I marked out the actual vantage points that I could draw from. After a week of such reconnaissance I was ready.

Give yourself a little time to allow the city to impose itself on you. (The bigger it is, the more time you will need.) Even if you are used to traveling, even if you feel at home in the bustle and confusion of a big city, you may not be accustomed to drawing under such conditions. If this is the case, it is much wiser to draw small towns until you can cope with city buildings—

Battery Park, New York City, 1964. (*Right*) *This handkerchief of a park seems dwarfed by the mixture of vintage skyscrapers, glass-box buildings and the unexpected Parisian Mansard-roofed United States Customs House. Drawn on Strathmore Script drawing paper with 6B and 7B Venus graphite pencils. From "New York: A City Destroying Itself,"* Panorama, 1965. *Courtesy Panorama, Milan, Italy.*

STATEN
ISLAND
FERRY →

Arnold's Pawnshop, South Street, Philadelphia, 1968.
(Above) The sugar-pink and scarlet front of Arnold's pawnshop made me stop to draw it. I used a 14" x 17" sketchbook of Alexis drawing paper with a Faber 702 sketching pencil. The house and the shop were painted with Faber Markettes; for signs and passing figures, I used a Spencerian nib and a Japanese brush with Higgins India ink. From "Hogarth's Philadelphia," Philadelphia Inquirer, March 9, 1969. Reproduced by permission of the owner, Frank B. Diamond, Philadelphia, Pennsylvania.

The Hotel Alexandra, Calgary, Alberta, Canada, 1969.
(Left) One of Calgary's oldest surviving hotels, the Alexandra, lies on the right side of the Canadian Pacific tracks. It is a great favorite with the cowboys whenever they hit town on spending sprees. I drew it one Sunday when things were quiet. Drawn in a 15" x 20" sketchbook of Glastonbury Antique paper with a Faber 702 sketching pencil and Faber Markettes. Touches of Winsor & Newton watercolors were painted with a No. 8 Winsor & Newton sable and a Japanese brush. An unpublished drawing from my own collection.

The Space Monument with Metro Station, Prospekt Mira, Moscow, U.S.S.R., 1967. *Modern city subjects often need the juxtaposition of active and passive elements to make them come alive. This obelisk commemorates the launching of the first earth satellite by the Russians. Drawn in a 15" x 20" sketchbook of Glastonbury Antique paper. An unpublished pencil and ink wash drawing from my Russian trip in 1967.*

singly or in groups—without feeling overwhelmed by noise or diverted by the attention of onlookers. Drawing smaller towns will enable you to adjust to working in a city more easily.

PRELIMINARY RESEARCH

Drawing is an artist's way of expressing a thought; it is his natural method of thinking. Nevertheless, in order to get started, I find a simple system essential. Before I start out on a trip, I read novels and magazine articles to help me obtain a clearer impression of my chosen city. I collect all kinds of clippings and take them along in a folder to read or refer to while I am on the road. Sometimes they prove to be unnecessary, but even then they have helped me to enter my subject.

A CONCEPTUAL APPROACH

Some cities offer such a wealth of material that it is very difficult to decide where you should begin. On such occasions you will need to approach your city in a more conceptual way. That is, you must select a *part* of the city that will enable you to convey the characteristic of the whole.

I had such a dilemma when I visited Morocco in August, 1971. Chuck Mee, the editor of *Horizon,* had accepted my idea for a portfolio about Fez, the old imperial capital of Morocco. Yet, when I arrived there—even though it was my second visit—I found such diversity that (even to my practiced eye) it was difficult to select a subject.

Palaces, gates, mosques—not to mention the maze of the Medina, the old quarter—vied for my attention. I realized that quickly I would have to find a unifying idea, a concept, if I was to complete the portfolio of twelve watercolor drawings in one week.

Driving on the panoramic highway that circled the city, I noted the profusion of monumental gateways (*bab* is the word for "gate" in Arabic) which provided entrances and exits to the complex inner districts. Not only did each gate have a distinctive architectural character, but its own variety of daily life taking place about it. My theme, I decided, would be "The Gates of Fez."

My next step—as I had no time to draw them

The Singel, Amsterdam, Holland, 1965. *A view from a bridge is very often the best way to see a city, particularly one like Amsterdam with its façades clustered along a maze of tree-lined old canals. Drawn with a 7B Venus graphite pencil in an 18¾" x 13½" Reeves sketchbook of cartridge paper. An unpublished drawing from my own collection.*

Coney Island Elevated, New York, 1962. *(Above)
Drawn on white Saunders paper with a Japanese
brush and a Spencerian school nib in Higgins manuscript ink. The figure with his foot on the fire hy-
drant is drawn with a 4B Venus graphite pencil.
From* Brendan Behan's New York, *1964. Courtesy
Hutchinson Publishing Group, London; and Bernard
Geis Associates, New York. Reproduced by permission of the owner, Randolph Bye, New Hope, Pennsylvania.*

Trafalgar Square, London, 1966. *(Right) Trafalgar
Square, heart of Britain and the Commonwealth, is
one of the finest sites in Europe for pigeons, getting
acquainted with the opposite sex, and street pho-
tographers. Drawn against the morning sun on a
sheet of Strathmore Script paper with a Faber 702
sketching pencil. From* London à la Mode, *1966.
Reproduced by permission of owners, the Lidice
Memorial Gallery, Lidice, Czechoslovakia.*

MORNING: TRAFALGAR SQUARE

Dublin Street Scene, 1964. *I am particularly empathetic to the bars, the shops, and the vaudeville theaters of the older decaying districts of a city. Like the faded charm of an old woman once beautiful, there's a great deal more to a city than meets the eye. Drawn with 3B and 7B Venus graphite pencils on a 16" x 20½" sheet of mold-made, cream-wove Saunders paper. Courtesy the Shelbourne Hotel, Dublin, Ireland.*

all—was to list those gates sufficiently different from each other. The obviously important ones I noted first. For example, *Bab Boujeloud* was the main entrance to the famous *souks,* or markets. *Bab Dkaken,* on the other hand, seemed like a backdrop for a country fair. All around it there were snake-charmers, peddlers, storytellers, and folk ensembles staging impromptu entertainments to a motley throng straight out of *The Arabian Nights.* Behind both gates were the minarets of mosques as well as a miscellany of ancient buildings from which I selected only those that suited my composition. Other gates were simply architecturally different, having round, square, or octagonal towers or cone- and wedge-shaped battlements. Exploiting such differences, whatever they were, enabled me to fully absorb the essential architectural quality of this immensely complex old city.

If you are interested in making a series or a portfolio about the city you were born or raised in (or better still a city that has cast its spell on you) there is no better way to help you digest and, therefore, more easily draw your subject than by searching out a unifying theme or concept.

NEIGHBORHOOD SUBJECTS

Of course, there is no reason for remaining downtown. One of the best ways of savoring a city is to look for a neighborhood district. I usually find that those dating from 1900–1920 are best. In such neighborhoods there is plenty of material for streetscapes or façades, such as a strip of shops with a church or a bar sandwiched in between them. Shops are particularly interesting, because they usually have plenty of signs. These are often of various vintages, as yet unreplaced by the more standardized modern kinds. I invariably draw such subjects—the much-loved corner sweetshop or that spooky-looking house—with a high degree of emotional involvement. I draw such places in almost every city I visit.

There are theaters and movies (the poor relations of those grand opera houses) and new, chromium-plated "art" movie houses. The old theaters and movie houses are unashamedly vernacular; with their fly-bitten posters of old movie stars, they make ideal subjects for a more nostalgic pencil. A city, in fact, can be so rich that you never need go outside it in search of subjects.

15
Commercial Vernacular Architecture

Architecture built in the commercial vernacular style is staunchly dedicated to the proposition that commerce, or rather the advertising of it, *must* run hog wild to bring in the customers. It has, therefore, its own good reasons for adopting an attitude of philistine contempt for any kind of taste. Yet its vigorous, earthy imagery rooted in the more indigenous forms of Victorian advertising art offers a huge variety of richly visual subject matter.

COMMERCIAL VERNACULAR ARCHITECTURE IN AMERICA

In a swiftly changing world this style thrives everywhere, but nowhere as luxuriantly as in the United States. This country possesses the conditions as well as the aggressive entrepreneurs essential for growth of such a style.

Commercial architecture changes from one region of America to another and is inspired by what is locally exploitable. I still think of a 1971 trip to Los Angeles where I discovered a riotous display of bizarre structures for "dining out." Like weeds in the hot sun of California, restaurants sprout up—some shaped like hats, milk cans, coke bottles, even owls.

Up in the Northwest, on the plains of Nebraska, in the hills and badlands of the Dakotas, in the wilds of Wyoming and Montana, right up to Alberta, Canada, a "pop western" style of commercial architecture holds sway. Giant cutout signs and billboards of Buffalo Bill Cody, Jim Bridger, General Custer, and Indian chiefs advertise a medley of fake forts, trading posts, motels, diners, and houses of yesterday. Invariably, I find them a delight to draw.

As deeply attached as I am to the Old West, top architectural honors in the commercial vernacular style must be given to Florida. Its artificial "Edens," seafood eateries, and space boom-towns are the ultimate in pop eccentricity and commercial "ballyhoo."

Galley Seafood, San Clemente, California, 1971. *(Right) I drew this piece of seaside commercial architecture one morning with a growing appetite for the specialty of the restaurant, an abalone "sandwitch." Drawn in about an hour with a Faber 702 sketching pencil, Grumbacher watercolors, and Higgins India ink. Courtesy Playboy magazine. © January, 1972, by Playboy magazine, Chicago, Illinois.*

Motel Sign, New Hampshire, 1963. *This was drawn shortly before I called it quits after a long day's driving and checked into "Indian Shutters" for a good night's rest. It was drawn in a 14" x 17" sketchbook of English cartridge paper with a Gillot 303 nib and Higgins India ink. An unpublished drawing from my own collection.*

For example, take Coco Beach, Florida. Incorporated in 1925, it has an area of five square miles with a population of 9,500 and a six-mile strip of reclaimed swamp flanking Ocean Highway. Kindled by America's space program from nearby Cape Kennedy, the city has spawned its own peculiar architectural idiom which can only be described as "space spectacular." The downtown section of Coco Beach is a sprawl of jerry-built supermarkets, dominated by "motel row," a jungle of cement-block inns topped with huge neon-lit, eye-smashing signs shaped like spacecraft, satellites, and guided missiles; these motels provide temporary quarters for visiting space specialists. Like the frontier towns of old America, almost everyone has helped build Coco Beach.

USING MIXED MEDIA

Because of its unorthodox and colorful character, architecture in the commercial vernacular has encouraged me to make far less conventional drawings and to try out new media.

In the autumn of 1965, I was in the American Northwest, drawing modern aspects of western life for the Strathmore Paper Company. I found plenty of material. One of my first subjects was Fort Cody in North Platte, Nebraska. This drawing was the starting point of my exploration with color markers. Built in the style of the old trading posts with roughly hewn pine logs, lookout towers, and cannons, the fort was graced by a huge cutout billboard of Buffalo Bill holding his favorite Winchester. The scene stopped me dead in my tracks. At once I realized that I would have to draw the subject in a much less formal way than the bridges and skyscrapers I had previously been working on further east.

For the first time I decided to use a combination of Faber 702 graphite pencil and Faber Markettes. I worked quickly with the markers over a pencil outline of Buffalo Bill. I enjoyed the sensation of drawing with the markers; they seemed like a pen, pencil, *and* brush all in one. I placed the fort itself in the background in isometric projection using strongly accented pencil strokes. The drawing did not work out quite as well as I had hoped, but it had enabled me to look at "straight" architecture in a much more relaxed way. From now on, I would view architecture as a painter views his subject—as large *shapes* of color. This color could be washes of ink, watercolor, or pencil.

PLANNING YOUR COMPOSITION

Because of its free-wheeling nature, architecture in the commercial vernacular often presents a multiplicity of very different, even conflicting, elements which somehow have to be related or fitted together to make a harmonious whole. Before you attempt larger and more ambitious drawings of this architectural style, spend a little time orienting yourself to your subject.

Select vantage points and work out the best perspective system or composition for your particular subject. A drawing has a far greater chance of going wrong if you do not take this extra effort and plan your moves with care. I spend as much as a half hour and more, whenever possible, working out a composition sketch. This sketch acts as a guide and reminds me of what I have to do next.

SEARCHING FOR A THEME

Back to Coco Beach, Florida for a typical example. I was looking around for a big "lead" subject for a portfolio I was doing for the *Daily Telegraph Magazine* during the Apollo 9 spaceshot of March 1969. I had thought of doing a double-page watercolor drawing. This large format would give me a good excuse to include some of the city's meaty motel "vernacular"; at the same time I could relate the community—that "dormitory" full of top scientists and engineers—to Cape Kennedy, whose launching pads were clearly visible on the skyline ten miles north.

I drove down Main Street which was also called Orlando Avenue and North Atlantic Avenue for part of its way through the town. Nothing hinted at the traditional role of a town; there was no sense of organic unity. In fact, it was very much the opposite. Motels, shopping centers, drive-ins, gas stations, and night spots were strung out along the streets like booths at a trade fair. Diverse and widely contrasting architectural idioms with an international flavor competed for the attention of drivers. The native motorists had become resistant to the blandishments of such advertising,

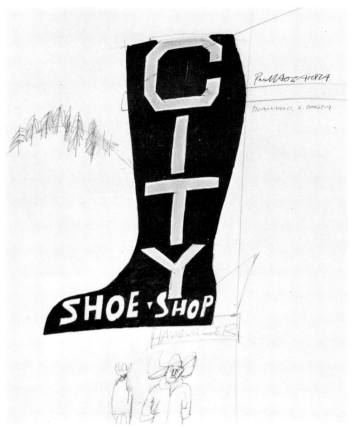

Shoe Shop Sign, Deadwood City, South Dakota, 1965. *This was also drawn with a Faber sketching pencil and Faber Markettes in an 11″ x 14″ sketchbook of Strathmore two-ply, medium surface drawing paper. Courtesy the Strathmore Paper Company, West Springfield, Massachusetts.*

Gateway to the Moonport: Coco Beach, Florida, 1969. *Because of its unorthodox, colorful character, the eye-smashing, vernacular architecture of Florida makes for far less conventional renderings. On a double-page spread of a 14" x 17" sketchbook of Strathmore Alexis paper, I drew the whole scene with a Faber 702 sketching pencil. Marubu watercolors with Nos. 6 and 9 Winsor & Newton sable brushes, and then Faber Markettes were used for the sky and those signs that needed stronger emphasis. Finally, the figures, the automobiles, and more signs were added with Spencerian and Gillot 303 nibs, a Japanese brush, and Higgins India ink. From "Reaching for the Moon from Coco Beach," Daily Telegraph Magazine, July 23, 1971. Courtesy Daily Telegraph Magazine, London, England.*

Brown Derby, Wilshire Boulevard, Hollywood, Los Angeles, 1971. *California vernacular architecture, on the other hand, celebrates the more bizarre with restaurants shaped like hats. For this one, I painted in sepia and green Winsor & Newton watercolors over a light pencil outline in a 15" x 20" sketchbook of Glastonbury Antique paper. An unpublished drawing from my own collection.*

Sioux Trading Post, Ogallala, Nebraska, 1965. *On the plains of Nebraska, in the hills of South Dakota, and even in the wilds of New Hampshire, Western vernacular architecture has always stopped me dead in my tracks, compelling me to get out my sketchbook and put it down. This huge, cut-out building was drawn with a Faber sketching pencil and Faber Markettes in an 11" x 14" sketchbook of Strathmore drawing paper. Courtesy the Strathmore Paper Company, West Springfield, Massachusetts.*

having been exposed to it since childhood. Although there was nowhere to walk, the vast asphalt parking lots made it easy to stop and look for a point from which to draw.

After the two trips up and down this six-mile strip, I eventually found a vantage point that gave me a good general view of the four-lane highway crowded with automobiles that ran to Cape Kennedy. I placed my horizon line up at the top of my sheet, taking the highway right up to the distant vanishing point of launch pads. This gave me plenty of room beneath for a whole battery of neon-lit signs. I drew these signs from different positions. These signs were often bigger than the establishments they advertised. Yet, I made them even bigger, leaving out the less bizarre ones in order to intensify the "free-for-all" ambiance.

SELECTING A FOCAL POINT

Even so, it became necessary to select one sign as a focal point to bring the others into line. I did not have to look very far. In front of me was the huge rotating globe of the Satellite Motel. The sign was mounted on a pillar which spelled out the flashing words, M-O-T-E-L; the sign's own neon-lit satellite orbitted above the words. I suppose it was the obvious choice, but, nevertheless, it proved to be a most appropriate symbol.

Then, I shifted around searching for other signs. I fitted them in like contrasting pieces in a sort of interlocking composition of vertical and horizontal shapes. The Koko Motel—disguised as a Japanese temple complete with wall garden—was placed against a "go-go" girlie night spot, which might have been inspired by an over-sized, Samoan tribal meeting-house. Gas stations surrounded by clusters of palm trees provided a welcome respite from such buildings but more motels had to follow, particularly those like the Sea Missile Motel which sported vast rockets.

Eagerly, almost boyishly, I continued to discover intriguing extras: a Chinese bridge which led nowhere; a Formica-chrome hamburger joint housed in a lunar module; plus a multiplicity of exhortations to eat, watch girls, bowl, dance, swim, and have cocktails in the Pillow Talk Lounge.

Two and a half hours later I succumbed to two of these exhortations: a swim and a char-broiled steak. After that drawing, I felt I had more than earned them!

The Timeless Occult Bookshop, Sunset Boulevard, Los Angeles, 1971. *This drawing was done with a Faber sketching pencil and Faber Markettes with touches of Grumbacher watercolor and Higgins India ink applied with Japanese brushes. An unpublished drawing from my own collection.*

16
Architecture and the Suburban Scene

Unlike the downtown districts of a city where you can walk, you more commonly drive through suburban "sprawl." At first sight, there appears to be little in the suburbs to engage your sympathy or your interest as possible subject matter. Yet there is something worth discovering and drawing in every suburb.

However, such discoveries have to be based on a higher and more personal level of visual awareness than is the case with historical architecture. It is far easier to look at, say, a baroque church in Vienna and feel certain that it is worthy of your pencil than it is to discover a subject in your own suburban neighborhood. In other words, you will need to develop an "approach" to drawing the suburbs because the more obvious esthetic considerations appear to be absent. Making something special out of the jumbled hodgepodge of London "Spanish," Brooklyn "Improved Shantytown," 1930's "Aztec," or ranchhouse "modern," presents a challenge to your graphic inventiveness.

BEGIN AWAY FROM HOME

I have found it much easier to develop the capacity to make such discoveries in suburban districts that are new to me. Vernacular architecture is that architecture done in an idiom indigenous or native to a particular city, region, or county. So the fascination of the totally unfamiliar can provide the impulse needed to see the most mundane building as a subject for drawing. Once you have acquired this capacity for observation, you can often return and see your own neighborhood with new eyes.

Springfield, Massachusetts, 1963. *(Right) Here I wanted to place a piece of industrial architecture—the Westinghouse plant—in a suburban setting. However, as I drove through the suburb, I found the vintage frame houses all scattered and unrelated to each other, as well as to the plant. So I created a composite drawing by selecting various elements from different locations and combining them into one drawing. Drawn on Saunders paper, in Higgins India ink and Grumbacher watercolors. Courtesy Fortune magazine. © December, 1963 by Time, Inc., New York.*

Thirteenth Avenue, Calgary, Alberta, Canada, 1969.
(Above) Southwestern Calgary with its clapboard
frame houses of the mid 1900's had a strong nostalgic appeal for me. The houses reminded me of
those on the postcards, mailed home by my father,
that are now in the family album. As a youngster of
nineteen, he had emigrated to Western Ontario in
1913. Drawn in a 15″ x 20″ sketchbook of Glastonbury Antique paper with a Faber 702 sketching
pencil. Blotted washes of Grumbacher watercolor
were used to paint in the faded colors of the houses;
Higgins India ink was used for the telegraph pole in
the foreground. Reproduced by permission of the
owner, Mrs. Manolsen, London, England.

Street Scene, Staten Island, New York, 1963. (Right)
The older suburbs with their ornate wooden frame
houses dating from the 1890's are goldmines of
hauntingly nostalgic material. I drew this house with
a Spencerian school nib, a Japanese brush, and
Higgins India ink on Saunders paper. From Brendan
Behan's New York, 1964. Courtesy Hutchinson Pub-
lishing Group, London; and Bernard Geis Associates,
New York. Reproduced by permission of the owner,
Christopher Walker, Cambridge, England.

Street Scene on STATEN ISLAND

Laurel Canyon, North Hollywood, Los Angeles, 1971. *(Above) This glimpse of suburban Hollywood was made with a combination of pencil, markers, and watercolors. First, an outline drawing was made with a Faber 702 sketching pencil. Then, I blocked in the hillsides with yellow and light green Faber Markettes. Details such as pine and cypress trees were painted in with undiluted Winsor & Newton viridian watercolor using a No. 6 Winsor & Newton sable brush. The palm trees were drawn in with a light green marker in a 15" x 20" sketchbook .of Glastonbury Antique drawing paper. An unpublished drawing from my own collection.*

Plaza Calvo Sotelo, Soller, Majorca, 1963. *(Right) Nothing much happens in Soller. People go about their everyday lives against the fabric of a 1900's provincial style of architecture which has great charm. Drawn in about an hour and a half with 3B and 7B Venus graphite pencils on mold-made, cream-wove Saunders writing paper. From Majorca Observed, 1965. Courtesy Cassell and Company, London; and Doubleday & Company, Inc., New York.*

Neighborhood Scene, Hollywood, California, 1971. *The fascination of unfamiliar neighborhoods can often generate an interest in subjects you might reject if you knew them well. Drawn with a Faber 702 sketching pencil and Faber Markettes (yellow, green, and orange) in an 11″ x 14″ sketchbook of two-ply, high-surface Strathmore drawing paper. An unpublished drawing from my own collection.*

NOSTALGIA AND THE ABSURD AS MOTIVATION

The unfamiliar in architecture can become even more magically irresistible when laced with nostalgia. My various encounters with the American suburban scene between 1962 and 1965 were enhanced by some half-recalled memories which were a constant source of inspiration.

I began drawing the older suburbs of Staten Island, New York, that dated from the earlier 1900's. They were a gold mine of material. The following year I moved on to the suburbs in Springfield, Massachusetts, that were built in the 1920's and 1930's; they were just as rich in their variety of wooden vernacular architecture. In the suburbs of both places, frame houses with their richly ornamented stoops and embellished turrets evoked images of the silent movies I had seen in my childhood.

On the other hand, suburban architecture of more recent vintage usually evokes a different reaction. Although nostalgia may be present in newer suburbs, I am usually bowled over by the proliferation of whimsical absurdities. Such ludicrous structures as a modern ranch house with wrought-iron gates, garden gnomes, and imitation medieval windows produce in me a compulsion to satirize; it is this response that becomes the motivating factor when drawing such scenes.

VANTAGE POINTS AND THE TIME OF DAY

The tree-lined streets of the suburbs are usually quite relaxing and afford plenty of places from which to draw. Therefore, I usually carry a much wider range of materials and equipment. I like to begin around ten o'clock in the morning when everyone is either at work or at school, and I generally use a car. At that time of day, suburban streets are quiet and I can cruise around unnoticed, looking for vantage points to draw from. I have a pocket-sized sketchbook on my lap to note possible subjects and street names, etc. Then, I can easily backtrack without having to ask my way and thus risk breaking my mood of reflection.

MAKING A COMPOSITE DRAWING

In a watercolor drawing of Springfield, Massachusetts, that I once did, I had the task of depicting a suburban district to the north of that city, close to a huge Westinghouse plant. Driving along St. James Avenue, I discovered all sorts of frame houses but all of them were scattered and visually unrelated to each other and to the plant that the suburb depended on. After I had driven around for about twenty minutes, I worked out an arrangement which would enable me to make as effective a composite drawing as possible.

Since no single vista provided me with a good composition, I invented one. I returned to four separate locations and selected various, interesting elements from each, starting with the plant. I combined all these interesting elements in one picture that said something more significant about that suburb than any single location would have done.

DRAWING FROM IMAGINATION AND MEMORIES

The final touch for this drawing was also provided by my imagination. I found myself adding a corner drugstore and coffee shop which almost line for line resembled the half-remembered newsstand and candy shop of my boyhood in the Manchester suburb of Longsight.

Remember to use your imagination. Make the suburban scene a point of departure for drawings of buildings that you associate with your childhood or recent past. As I have suggested, you can imbue the apparent absurdity of these buildings with a comment based on your own feelings (love or hatred) about them. You will soon begin to look twice at the suburban scene, possibly your own, and discover that it is a rich source of material.

17
Architecture and Landscape

In relation to architecture, landscape only concerns me when it can form a contrast or setting for a building or group of buildings. I am only impressed with the grace and strength of a forest or a mountain if it will enable me to develop the pictorial impact or the social significance, or both, of my architectural drawing. For example, the personality of a farm functions in a completely different way if I can invest it with something of the restlessness of nature that surrounds it.

OBSERVING LANDSCAPE

My feeling for landscape in an architectural context always comes about by giving myself a little time to get used to what is actually present. Sometimes the landscape predominates; at other times it will be the architecture. That is my first decision: whether one is going to be bigger than the other. Next, I scan the terrain to see what elements are present—man-made and natural—that might work well together. I will think of ways to organize or regroup scattered elements.

For instance, I may be struck by a landscape with olive groves outlining the shape of a mountain. It may *look* good, but will it make a good drawing? In reflection, I decide that it may turn out to be a little monotonous. So I continue looking around to see what other elements might be related to one another to form a drawing: a lonely villa dominated by a massive, threatening mountain; an engraved milestone set against a huge verdant thicket of bamboo; and an artesian well that is black and rusting against the texture of slanting grass. I always find that the clues to a dramatic composition are there—all I have to do is to follow them and work out ideas. So I usually try and spend at least fifteen minutes, if not more, taking in my surroundings, observing aspects of landscapes and architecture. Such reflections enable me to visualize an effective image.

Arta, Majorca, 1964. *(Right) A Moorish-style house and the distant village are set against a thickly wooded hillside. Drawn entirely with 5B and 7B Venus graphite pencils on a 20" x 16½" sheet of white Saunders paper. From Majorca Observed, 1965. Courtesy Cassell and Company, London; and Doubleday & Company, Inc., New York.*

ARTA PaulHogarth '64

The Catskills at Palenville, New York, 1963. *(Above) This watercolor drawing was made with quite a mixture of media. The village store, highway sign, parked automobile, and passing figures were all drawn with a Gillot 303 nib and Higgins India ink. The sharply defined Victorian Gothic house was drawn with a Gillot 290 nib, a Winsor & Newton No. 6 sable brush, and a textured blotter. The landscape itself was painted on Saunders paper in Pelikan watercolors with a Japanese brush and Winsor & Newton Nos. 5 and 8 sable brushes. Trees in the foreground were rendered with a 6B Venus graphite pencil. Reproduced by permission of the owner, Charles Reid, Greens Farms, Connecticut.*

Windmills near Palma, Majorca, 1963. *(Right) A landscape setting enhances these old windmills of various vintages on the Plain of San Jorge. Drawn with Gillot 404 and 290 nibs using Higgins India ink on a 20″ x 16½″ sheet of white Saunders paper. From Majorca Observed, 1965. Courtesy Cassell and Company, London; and Doubleday & Company, Inc., New York.*

Swift Mausoleum at
Castlerick

Swift Mausoleum, Castlerick, Ireland, 1969. *(Left) Egyptian-style mausoleums were all the rage in late eighteenth-century Great Britain. This one commemorates Dean (Gulliver's Travels) Swift. Drawn with a Faber 702 sketching pencil and Higgins India ink. Reprinted from Lithopinion 16. © 1969 by Local One, Amalgamated Lithographers of America, New York.*

Szlembark, Poland, 1953. *(Above) Rural buildings, particularly those of eastern Europe, lend themselves to a natural setting. I used a background of tall trees for this village street in the highlands of Southern Poland. Drawn with a soft Hardtmuth charcoal lead on Abbey Mill poster paper. From Drawings of Poland, 1954. Courtesy Wydawnictwo Artystczno-Graficzne, Warsaw, Poland.*

Aloxe-Corton

UNIFYING ELEMENTS AND COMPOSITION

For example, some years ago I was out drawing landscape in Majorca. I was exploring the rich farms of the island's central plain; I was anxious to discover architectural motifs in the landscape which would help me comment on this land's gentle yet exotic flavor. Although hot, there was a slight breeze. Windmills turned and squeaked on each farm. I noticed that while each of the tiny farms was more or less the same—both in size, style, and shape—each windmill was completely different. One was circular with an overhanging, crenellated tower; a second was square with an incised diamond-shaped frieze across its top; a third looked like a chess pawn with no other feature but a loophole.

The analogy with chess gave me a clue to composition. I set the windmills out like a chessboard and drew them flanked by their respective farms and strips of cultivated earth. Here and there I included palm trees and a figure of a farm worker on his way to work.

Whatever type of subject matter I choose, I aim for a lively, stylized composition. It may not always come off, but at least it is essentially my own reaction to the subject. Try to avoid the temptation to sentimentalize about inherently picturesque subjects. Control your affection for farms and churches in landscape by concentrating more on their esthetic qualities in terms of your chosen medium. Try to think more conceptually to develop a composition. Do not be afraid to impose your imagination on your subject.

COMBINING TOWN AND COUNTRYSIDE

Sometimes I will combine townscape with landscape. Here the problem is different. Some knowledge of a place helps, even if you have not been there before. During the summer of 1969, I found a particularly good subject, the town of High River in southern Alberta (page 104). As in most of the frontier towns that grew up around the tracks of the Canadian Pacific Railway, this town was built around the railway depot. Every building obviously owed its existence to the rich grain and stock country which lay on every side as far as the eye could see.

I noticed that on one side of the town lay three sentinel-like grain elevators nestling close to the Canadian Pacific depot. On the other was the business district—a straggling line of banks, streets, and hotels built in vernacular Western style. The big open sky above and an ocean-like plain of wavering wheat and grass dominated everything.

A good viewpoint was important because I had to judge carefully this relationship of sky and fields to the town. I found one between the railroad tracks and the main street and settled down to get the architectural part of my drawing done. I used a scissor-like composition based on the railway tracks and the street, and I grouped the grain elevators on one side and the row of buildings on the other. Then, I moved to another viewpoint to get a closer look at the landscape. It was vast. To help convey its vastness, I let the railroad line vanish across the open plain, right off the paper.

Chateau de Saissey, Aloxe Corton, France, 1970. *A nineteenth-century chateau in the Côte de Beaune, Burgundy blends pleasantly with a landscape of vineyards. Drawn and painted in a 15" x 20" sketchbook of Glastonbury Antique drawing paper with a Faber 702 sketching pencil, Winsor & Newton watercolors, and Nos. 5 and 9 Winsor & Newton sable brushes. From "Three Glorious Days of Burgundian Bacchanalia," for the* Daily Telegraph Magazine, *London, September 17, 1971. Reproduced by permission of the owners, Mr. and Mrs. Kenneth Twist, Cambridge, England.*

18
Using Architecture in Illustration

Having talked about drawing architecture at such length, it seems logical that I should also discuss drawing architecture in relation to illustration.

In one form or another, a knowledge of architecture is applicable to every type of editorial and advertising art. Look at the illustrations in this chapter alone. These will give you some idea of the wide range of possibilities.

THE DEMANDS OF HISTORICAL ILLUSTRATION

In general, illustration invariably compels me to interpret an art director's or editor's instructions. Therefore, I have to fulfill certain special requirements while, at the same time, adding my own comments. This almost certainly requires me to read the manuscript that I will be illustrating. I must submerge myself in what may well be the life and look of a certain time, possibly two or even four centuries ago. At first, this will be a tedious process, but as I continue I will become completely absorbed, grasping the implications of the story and its leading and supporting characters.

At this initial stage, what invariably makes all the difference is having a general idea of the physical context of the period. If you can visualize the architecture of the period you are well on the way to finding the pictorial means to effectively illustrate the story. In other words, you have to be aware of a period's distinguishing physical characteristics in order to recreate something of its original flavor.

Therefore, an illustration of a historical event seems to emerge as much from an intimate acquaintance with the architecture of the period as it does from a personal feeling for the narrative I am illustrating.

RESEARCHING BACKGROUND INFORMATION

In 1964, one of my historical assignments was an eight-page portfolio of paintings for a special Shakespeare issue of *Life*. The assignment required an in-depth study of the Elizabethan Age—its architecture as well as events and people. Without doubt, if I had not already drawn architecture (not necessarily Tudor) on location, I would have found the task much more formidable.

Stratford-on-Avon, England in Elizabethan times. *This illustration—the opening spread —was originally reproduced by letterpress in color. It is one of a series made in 1964, and depicts bustling Stratford, the birthplace of William Shakespeare, on market day. Drawn with Caran d'Ache charcoal lead, 4B and 6B Eagle Charco pencils, and 6B Venus graphite pencil, and augmented with passages of Winsor & Newton gouache color on Hollingworth Kent Mill paper. From the special Shakespeare number of* Life, *April 23, 1964*. © *Time Inc., New York. Reproduced by permission of the owner, Lane Fortinberry, New York.*

Book Jacket Illustration, 1965. *This illustration includes three examples of seventeenth-century English village architecture transplanted to New England. I based my drawing primarily on references found in the text of Mr. Powell's book. I had known and drawn—and even lived—in such houses in England. The original drawing, roughly twice as large, was done in line and wash with Higgins India ink and both a Gillot 303 nib and a Japanese brush. Courtesy Doubleday & Company, Inc., New York.*

Book Jacket Illustration, 1967. *This drawing of a Victorian mill was based on an earlier one I did of the old Underwood Typewriter plant at Hartford, Connecticut, while on a Fortune assignment in 1963. I compressed the original building's shape and left out unnecessary details. I concentrated on conveying the inhuman character of Victorian industrial plants. Drawn in Higgins India ink with a Japanese brush and a Gillot 303 nib. Courtesy Doubleday & Company, Inc., New York.*

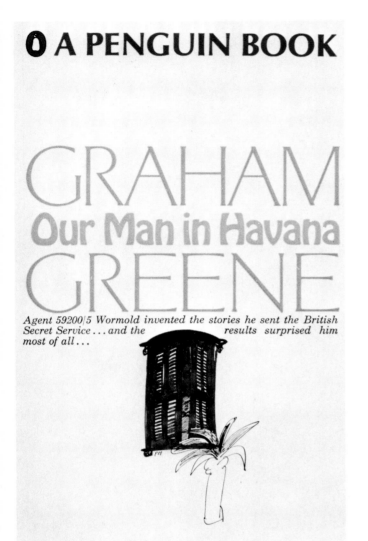

O A PENGUIN BOOK

GRAHAM
Our Man in Havana
GREENE

Agent 59200/5 Wormold invented the stories he sent the British Secret Service...and the results surprised him most of all...

Book Jacket Illustration, 1968. *By reading the text of the novel I am going to illustrate, I glean the specifics of the story's time and place. Then I can intensify the ambiance of the novel by selecting and illustrating details that evoke these specifics. Here I tried to suggest the intrigue and mystery of the story with a mysterious face peering from behind partly closed, Caribbean-type shutters. Courtesy Penguin Books, London and Baltimore.*

My opening illustration, a large double spread, was to be a bucolic and bustling townscape packed with all the exuberance of English life at that time. Stratford-on-Avon was a well ordered little town in Elizabethan days and Shakespeare's father was its town constable, tax collector, ale taster *and* high bailiff. Almost every detail of the manuscript could be related to the architecture of that period.

William himself was born in a rambling old, gabled house. He was baptized and later buried in Trinity Church; he worshipped in the Guild Chapel and studied Latin in the schoolroom over the long Guild Hall. All these buildings obviously had to be included in the townscape which I decided had to be a semipanoramic composite view of the town on market day. This townscape would also include a landscape of fields and riverbanks where men were hunting, hawking, and fishing.

Research material was sent to me, including photostats and photographs of engravings and woodcuts of Elizabethan buildings of every kind. I added a few of my own on-the-spot observations, having something of the excitement and colorful spectacle of an actual English market day in the nearby country town of Sudbury, Suffolk.

PRELIMINARY SKETCHES

Eventually, I set to work, making preliminary scribbles; then I did sketches on a pad of tracing paper with a 6B Venus graphite pencil. With the general idea of the composition growing in my head, I scaled the working area to about half up on the reproduced size of 13½″ × 15½″ (35 × 27 cm.) Using a sheet of good quality tracing paper cut from a 36″ (89 cm.) roll, I began to develop the composition in detail, starting with the buildings around the market place. I worked back to the horizon with rows of houses, churches, and finally a landscape of meadows and wooded hills.

Once the general setting was complete, I began to evolve the details of each building, exploiting such characteristic Elizabethan features as timber framing, mullioned windows and half-hipped roofs. To anchor what had now become a medley of medieval and Elizabethan inns, houses, cottages, shops, guild-

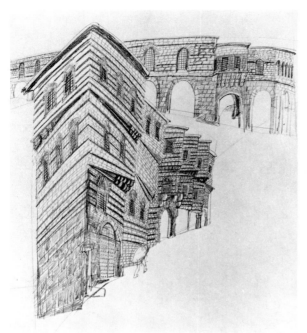

Byzantine Warehouses, Istanbul, 1966. *(Preliminary Version) This drawing was part of a series devoted to life in twelfth-century Constantinople. Drawn with a Faber 702 pencil supplemented with 3B and 5B graphite pencils for precise detail.*

Byzantine Warehouses, Istanbul, 1966. *(Final Version) I completed the drawing by adding the caravan traffic. From Byzantium, a volume in the "Great Ages of Man" series, Time-Life Books. © 1966, Time, Inc., New York.*

Juarez as a Young Lawyer, 1968. *This double-page drawing was done in pen and ink wash for a child's book about Mexico's struggle for independence. I was concerned with conveying the atmosphere of the small provincial town (Oaxaca) where young Juarez practiced law, as well as implying that this was a temporary period in his long and eventful career. The buildings were drawn from photographs. From* Out from Under, *by James D. Atwater and Ramon E. Ruiz, 1969. Courtesy Zenith Books, Doubleday & Company, Inc., New York.*

Lavenham, Suffolk, England, 1966. *I almost always ignore true perspective. I prefer an arrangement that enables me to freely interpret shapes and textures in a relaxed and fluent way. If I want to emphasize one building against another, I make the ones behind smaller and smaller. Drawn with a Faber 702 pencil with touches of Winsor & Newton watercolor and Higgins India ink, in a custom-made 15″ x 20″ sketchbook of Glastonbury Antique laid drawing paper. An unpublished drawing from my own collection.*

halls, almshouses, churches, and chapels, I used the market cross with its tiled roof, cupola, and weather vane as a focal point.

THE FINAL DRAWING

Having obtained the approval of the art director, Bernie Quint, to go ahead, once both the idea and the composition were fully worked out, it took about fourteen hours to complete the final art. I placed the working drawing on a light box and traced in its main outlines with a 4B pencil; then I switched to a soft Hardt-muth charcoal lead and Caran d'Ache charcoal lead to develop the drawing with a vigorous and bold line. Washes of watercolor were then laid over all the buildings to gradually boost and emphasize the fairy tale character of Tudor architecture and its use of tawny hues.

When the washes were dry, more color passages were added with a No. 3 sable brush. I used stronger mixtures of pure color, then blotted them to simulate the blistered, textured effects on walls and roofs of the building. After completing the architectural background, the drawing progressed upwards to a deer hunt, hawking with falcons, and men trout-fishing. Towards the middle of the drawing the attention shifted to a group of townsfolk who were shopping, talking, quarreling, or just going about their various daily routines. Finally, I worked over the color washes for the third time strengthening wherever necessary.

ILLUSTRATING ARCHITECTURE FOR CHILDREN'S BOOKS

Nominally, children's books are for children. However, the artists who illustrate them do not mind if adults, or anyone else, read them. Whether children's books concern fables on a grand scale, such as conflicts between the sun and the moon (or two rival corporations), or whether they are just about witches, animals, and fairies, they are bound to involve the use of architectural backgrounds of one kind or another. Children of all ages love plenty of action and well-defined movement. When I illustrate children's books, I make sure that this action goes on against a background that is equally as colorful and detailed.

ILLUSTRATING ARCHITECTURE FOR FICTION

My use of architecture in adult fiction, on the other hand, is mostly confined to jacket drawings for paperback reprints of modern novels. For such drawings I will use architectural details of a specific period or style. I can relate these details in a dramatic way to characters, or the story's ambiance.

Such details can range from a door handle to an ivy-clad college wall. For example, I might, as I did for a Penguin edition of Graham Greene's *Our Man in Havana,* use ornate Car-ribbean-type shutters as a setting; on this particular jacket, these shutters open slightly to permit an enigmatic face, hinting of the mystery and the intrigue of Cuba in the 1930's.

I evolve such combinations of architectural detail and characterization partly out of reading the text; such details may be fully described by the author. Sometimes I take the liberty of introducing them myself, because I know they would have existed in the situation that the narrative describes.

ILLUSTRATING ARCHITECTURE FOR NONFICTION

When illustrating nonfiction I usually allow the documentary part of the drawing to predominate. I will probably include a whole building rather than a detail. For example, in the jacket drawing for *Labouring Men* (a Doubleday Anchor paperback by historian Eric Hobsbawm concerning the history of labor struggles in the nineteenth century), I evolved a background image of a grim Victorian textile mill. I intensified its grimness by making it look more like a prison than a place of work. Based on an appreciation of their characteristics, I will use such buildings like symbols.

ORGANIZING AN ARCHITECTURAL "MORGUE"

On some illustration assignments I may not always be able to go out and make location studies of buildings. Also, the assignment may not justify the services of a commercial picture archive. To develop rough memory sketches into working drawings, and then final art, I usually work from reproductions and photographs. I clip them from newspapers and magazines, or I use my own reference library of

The Calgary Stampede: Main Entrance, Calgary, Canada, 1969. *If I have to illustrate an event, the appropriate architectural background often helps to establish a sense of place or occasion. Here, I used the reconstructed Northwest Mounted Police post, Fort Calgary, to convey the carnival mood of the annual ten-day stampede. Drawn with a Faber 702 sketching pencil and Faber Design Markettes in a custom-made 15" x 20" sketchbook of Glastonbury Antique drawing paper. Touches of Grumbacher watercolor were applied with a Japanese brush over the figures and the tepee in the foreground. Courtesy Sports Illustrated, July 13, 1970. Reproduced by permission of the owners, the Riveredge Foundation, Calgary, Alberta, Canada.*

USING ARCHITECTURE IN ILLUSTRATION   171

Reportorial Illustration, 1971. *The physical context of an event is as important as the event itself, particularly in a "lead" or opening illustration where the reader is exposed to the full flavor of the occasion. This watercolor painting was a double-page spread; it features the main event of the Royal Dublin Spring Show against the background of the Ballsbridge showgrounds. Drawn with a Faber 702 sketching pencil and painted with Faber Markettes and Winsor & Newton watercolors on a 15" x 20" double sheet from a custom-made sketchbook of Glastonbury Antique paper. From portfolio on the Royal Dublin Society for the Smithsonian magazine, August, 1971. © Smithsonian Institution, Washington, D.C.*

books devoted to periods and styles of architecture. On these occasions, my "morgue" or reference files and books can be indispensable; they can save a great deal of time and energy.

Also a "morgue" of clippings will get me started sometimes and actually spark off an idea. Just turning over the pages of an old encyclopedia or illustrated history might give me some much-needed insight into a given period of history. There is a limit to the number of books you can collect, particularly expensive books on architecture. So you may find, as I do, that essentially your "morgue" should concentrate on a basic collection of clippings conveniently housed in box-files or folders.

However, box-files and folders do pose something of a storage problem, particularly if you are—as I am—an inveterate collector of books, old furniture, and anything that looks interesting. In recent years I have found it much more space-saving as well as time-saving to restrict my collection of significant examples of the world's architecture to postcards or 35mm color slides which can be conveniently stored in much smaller boxes and indexed for quick reference.

My own architectural "morgue" is confined to the main periods: early antiquity, Egyptian, classical (Greece and Rome), Romanesque, Islamic, Gothic, Renaissance, baroque, rococo, Victorian (early, middle and late), Art Nouveau, and the various periods of the modern movement before and after World Wars I and II. These periods will be represented by postcards, street lamps, doors, windows, etc., of each period. I will also have postcards on different types of ornaments, although I have found these largely unnecessary since Dover brought out their paperback edition of the already mentioned *Handbook of Ornament* by Franz Sales Meyer.

OTHER REFERENCE SOURCES

If my "morgue" does not help with a particular assignment (and sometimes it does not) I obtain more detailed references from a commercial picture archive. However, I will only use these if I have no alternative, because their fees can be high.

Sometimes my client may be good enough to provide well-documented picture material without charge. Time-Life Inc., in the United States, and the British Publishing Corporation, in Britain, are exceptional in that they like to make sure that illustrators work from authentic references when working for their historical books. Therefore, they have a full-time research staff to locate and provide such information for the writers and artists working on their projects.

Finally, drawing architecture for a particular illustration assignment demands an awareness of the physical characteristics of the past and the present. The characters in an historical essay, a children's story, or a novel for adults require authentic settings. Here, your knowledge will actively help your imagination to work more smoothly in order to recreate and reconstruct these various settings. Architecture is, more often than not, the skeletal framework of such illustration.

19
Drawing Interiors

Once you are familiar with the essentials of drawing architecture from the outside, it is only a small step to apply what you learn to the task of drawing architecture from the inside. I say *learn,* in the present tense, because drawing the interior of a building should be undertaken in conjunction with seeing or appreciating it from the outside.

SELECTION AND INTERPRETATION

Generally speaking, the problems are very much the same as those encountered when drawing the exteriors of buildings. There is, of course, the same need for cultivating an appreciation of style; this appreciation, in turn, provides the stimulus for attempting an interpretation of a building. There is also the need for selection. You must be able to select that which is strictly necessary from an interior. Above all, there is the need to roam around inside a building to get some ideas of *how* you might draw it before you actually put pencil to paper.

As in drawing architecture from the outside, the degree to which you make your imagination work is the key to a successful effective drawing. How you, yourself, see or react to the atmosphere, the flavor of an interior—whatever its style and purpose—will inevitably help you find a way to depict it. All you need to have is a healthy curiosity (preferably an insatiable one).

DRAWING "GUM"

For example, I spent much time tramping around what has to be the biggest Victorian-

Inside the "GUM" Department Store, Moscow, 1969. *(Right) All other department stores pale beside the Gosodarstveny Universalny Magazin, or State Universal Store, locally known as just "Goom." It is a vast Victorian complex reminiscent of an oriental bazaar; it is open seven days a week from eight in the morning to eight at night, jammed full with shoppers. The unique features of its interior are the iron stairways, balconies and bridges which join three vast floors. This pencil drawing is but one section; there are, in fact, fifty! Drawn with a Faber 702 sketching pencil in a 15" x 20" sketchbook of Glastonbury Antique drawing paper. From A Russian Journey: from Suzdal to Samarkand, 1969. Courtesy Cassell and Company, London; and Hill & Wang, Inc., New York.*

Moscow: GUM
Department Store

Tasting the New Wine: Cellars of the Hospices de Beaune, France, 1970. *Awareness of architecture frequently helps me compose interior scenes which have to include figures. Drawn with a Faber 702 sketching pencil in a 15″ x 20″ sketchbook of Glastonbury Antique paper. From "Three Glorious Days of Burgundian Bacchanalia," for the* Daily Telegraph Magazine, *September 17, 1971. Courtesy Daily Telegraph Magazine, London, England.*

style department store in the world, Moscow's *Gosodarstveny Universalny Magazin,* or State Department Store, or as Muscovites themselves call the place, GUM (pronounced *Goom*). To my western eyes GUM was both strange and remarkable. To my artist's eyes, however, it was a godsend—a natural subject for an architectural interior with all the trimmings.

The place was as different from Macy's or Harrods—or even Woolworth's—as I could possibly imagine. To begin with, the whole outside looked like a barracks big enough for a whole army including a tank division; it presents a façade with no apparent entrance or exit. Nor does this starkly unprepossessing frontage display any signs, shingles, billboards, or indeed any clue whatsoever which would lead you to suspect its extraordinary interior. Turning the corner at one end of it, I suddenly found myself being swept inside by a hurrying multitude reminiscent of Grand Central Station during the height of the Christmas shopping rush.

Once inside, the whole interior took my breath away; I was back in the 1890's, the years of its construction. Hugely ornate iron staircases, bridges, and balconies joined and linked three vast floors each three blocks in length and two in width. These bridges and balconies created the effect of an enormous labyrinth of fire escapes filled with scurrying shoppers in search of what appeared to be nonexistent merchandise. Suddenly conscious of what might be above, my glance traveled upward and fixed itself on an enormous canopy of glass supported by cast-iron pillars of gargantuan proportions. Like London's famous Crystal Palace, the design had obviously been planned around the largest piece of glass that could possibly have been made.

Clearly, the interior of this fantastic emporium was far too big a subject to take on without some careful thought. So after looking around for a while, I selected a part of it in a single vertical section. Like a slice of cake, this section enabled me to sample the contents of this interior without actually having to draw the whole thing. I chose a vantage point on the third floor from which I looked down one of the open balconies onto the floors below. Then I fixed a vanishing point towards the top center of my sketchbook page, widening the lines top and bottom to permit an almost bird's-eye view. After coping with a tenacious peasant woman who kept asking where the men's underwear department might possibly be, I finally added a section of the glass canopy; I made a free, Japanese kite-like shape of the glass to complement the crowded scene below.

INTERIORS AS IMAGINATIVE EXERCISES

The practice of drawing interiors can extend the range of your architectural vocabulary to such a remarkable extent that I highly recommend it for drawing architecture in general. I have found that using whatever time I had to draw interiors—due to bad weather or a bad mood—was a most effective way of evolving subjects out of a widening range of what appeared to be unprepossessing settings.

Cultivate the habit of looking inside a building before or after you have drawn its exterior. By helping you see the building as a whole, drawing interiors will help you increase your facility to draw its exteriors.

The Interior of St. Eirene, Istanbul, Turkey, 1966. *I selected only what was strictly necessary to convey the devout faith of these early Christians, in this unused illustration for the series depicting life in the former capital of the Byzantine Empire. The original drawing was made on location. When I re-drew it, I added the figures and the candelabra. I used a Faber 702 sketching pencil on Daler paper. Courtesy Time, Inc., New York.*

20 Random Notes

Various points or techniques which have a useful bearing on drawing architecture may not have been discussed in detail or may have been overlooked, until now. So they are all here, in one convenient place—my concluding chapter.

PROPORTION

Drawing buildings, particularly those full of complex or ornate detail, often presents a formidable task to the beginner. If it is any consolation, it is not all that much easier for me either! I think of each building as representative of a particular problem which has to be chewed over before I put pencil to paper. I observe the building's height and width and the shape it makes.

Next, I divide the building into subdivisions —columns, floors, etc. Again, I determine the height and width of each floor or column before I can go ahead and draw windows and doors in detail. I always try to ensure that everything, or at least most of it, is in place before I get down to details.

Sometimes I will find that there is no room for that fifth window, column, or chimney! On such occasions (and they happen frequently) I will have a pang of conscience until I remember that, after all, I am an artist interpreting architecture, not a photographer shooting it strictly for the record.

SCALE

A sense of scale is important, unless you want your drawing to turn out to be an octopus consuming every inch of the paper. This invariably happens if you allow yourself to be carried away with detail. Avoid this by developing a clear idea of how much of the building you want to draw in the first place. For example, if you want to draw the whole building, it will obviously occupy a much smaller area of your sketchpad than half the building. Accordingly, you must put more space between the building and yourself, or as I sometimes do, get close up to it.

WINDOWS

Windows always seem to be a headache because of the risk of making them stand out

High Holborn Street Scene, London, 1965. *This is one of central London's few remaining examples of Elizabethan architecture. It forms a row of shops and houses and looks like Noah's Ark in contrast to the straight lines of an adjacent new highrise office block. Drawn with a Faber 702 sketching pencil in a 10¾" x 14½" English Planet sketchbook of smooth drawing paper. From* London à la Mode, *1966. Courtesy Studio Vista, Ltd., London; and Hill & Wang, Inc., New York.*

Construction Scene, 53 Street and Sixth Avenue, New York, 1964. *(Left) This rising office block is being built on the site of demolished Victorian brownstones and threatens another nearby. It also destroys the scale of this once residential neighborhood. Drawn with a Faber 702 sketching pencil on Strathmore Script paper. From "New York: A City Destroying itself,"* Panorama, 1965. *Courtesy Panorama, Milan, Italy.*

White Horse Tavern, New York City, 1962. *(Above) Bars and taverns offer a welcome break from drawing grand architecture as well as providing refreshment at the end of the long day. The tavern's front was drawn with a Winsor & Newton No. 6 sable brush and blotted Higgins India ink; the rest of the building was done with a Gillot 404 nib, all on a Strathmore Alexis layout pad. From Brendan Behan's* New York, 1964. *Courtesy Hutchinson Publishing Group, London; and Bernard Geis Associates, New York.*

The Statue of Liberty, New York Harbor, 1962. *The sightseeing helicopters buzzing about give this view of the famous statue a piquancy it otherwise would not have possessed. Drawn with 5B and 7B Venus graphite pencils on Saunders paper. From Brendan Behan's New York, 1964. Courtesy Hutchinson Publishing Group, London; and Bernard Geis Associates, New York. Reprinted by permission of the owners, Library of Congress, Washington, D.C.*

The Bronze Maidens, Shelbourne Hotel, Dublin, 1964. *The plebeian perkiness of a girl newsvendor helps reveal the exotic flavor of the bronze maidens (known locally as "The Last Virgins"). They illuminate the front entrance of the celebrated hotel. Drawn with 5B and 7B Venus graphite pencils on Saunders paper. Courtesy the Shelbourne Hotel, Dublin, Ireland.*

too much or not at all. They can also be tedious to draw, particularly in Georgian (Federal) buildings because there are so many! Yet you cannot ignore them because they do play such an important part in establishing the style of the building.

Think of windows as holes, darker in tone than the outside wall. Only at night when a room is lit does the reverse apply. This simple priority will enable you to give window frames and sills the proper degree of emphasis.

PEOPLE AND BUILDINGS

Often a streetscape, a single building, or a part of a building can be dramatically improved by including a few people who seem to fit in—to be a part of the place. Such figures can contribute a great deal to drawings of architecture simply because they help establish the building's character and give a sense of time or place. Do not include everyone because they happen to be there. On the other hand, if they are not there to begin with, then wait for them. Select only those figures who will contribute to your picture, because they are interesting or significant in some comic or enigmatic way.

For example, in a large pencil and wash drawing I made of Trinity College, Dublin in 1968, I included figures of undergraduates walking to and from lectures, in pairs, in groups, or as figures. Although I had seen only a handful of students in the quadrangle by the Campanile, they were too good to leave out. They were so much a part of the subject, and besides they provided welcome visual relief from the severe lines and façades of the Georgian college buildings.

A word of warning. Until you have had plenty of practice, avoid drawing such figures off the cuff. You may place them in the wrong position; or worse still spoil an otherwise successful picture! On the other hand, you can always transcribe a figure sketched rapidly in a pocket notebook into the more detailed drawing later on. Then you can place the figure where it looks most effective.

OPPOSITES AND CONTRASTS

Juxtaposing old against new, or conventional against unconventional, often transforms a drawing which otherwise would be destined for the trash basket. I remember once making an elaborate pencil drawing of the Statue of Liberty. But after having done so, I said to myself, "So what?" Somewhere I had missed the mark. My drawing lacked tension even though I had well defined the statue's superbly earthy quality to my satisfaction.

I laid the drawing aside and looked at the tiny heads of the tourists trooping around her tiara. Then, after a while, I noticed the helicopters and tiny airplanes buzzing around her. This was exactly what I wanted, so I put in one of each kind of aircraft for maximum contrast. By doing so, I not only brought out the symbolical character of the huge statue but also added a light-hearted touch.

BARS AND TAVERNS

Bars and taverns, or pubs (public-houses) as they are called in Britain, offer façades of conviviality in every style. In big cities they differ greatly from those in small towns and villages. New York, for example, has almost every kind of bar, ranging from the seaport taverns of Brooklyn to 1930's German *staubes* in Yorkville and Victorian Irish saloons on Third Avenue. Then, there are the clapboard inns that line the ports of New England from Maine to Massachusetts, and those long brassy bars of the Old West, like those in Leadville, Colorado.

DRAWING ARCHITECTURE FROM PHOTOGRAPHS

There are times when, for one reason or another, it may not be possible to draw buildings on location. The only alternative is to draw them from photographs or clippings.

I do this in the following manner. I begin as though I was working on location, reacting to the subject as much as possible in the same way. I use what I see as a basis for developing my own interpretation. Therefore, I make my drawing as directly as possible, just as if the building was there in front of me. In this way, I can usually overcome the common danger of working from photographs—the feeling that the camera is imposing *its* decisions on you, instead of allowing you to make your own.

Glossary of Architectural Terms

Abacus. The flat slab on top of a capital on which the architrave rests.

Acanthus. Ornament based on the leaf of a thistle. It is used on composite and Corinthian capitals.

Alcove. Small projecting extension of an outer wall, always with windows, and usually decorative.

Arcade. A row or group of arches resting on pillars or columns.

Architrave. Horizontal main beam over columns.

Apse. End of a church, usually semicircular or polygonal.

Arch. Curved structure of wedge-shaped blocks of brick or stone held together by common pressure.

Arrow Loophole. Narrow vertical slit or opening, deeply splayed inside, in the walls or battlements of a castle. Arrows were shot through them.

Art Nouveau. Style of architecture and interior decoration using flat or three-dimensional writhing plant and animal forms based on a recognizable conception rather than a formalized or abstract decoration. See Mario Amaya's *Art Nouveau* (London and New York, 1966) for an introductory pictorial survey of movement. Nikolaus Pevsner's *Pioneers of Modern Design* (London and Baltimore, 1960) contains more details of architectural achievements.

Baluster. Small bulging column, usually bottle-shaped, that supports a parapet.

Barbican. An outer defense usually set between the towers of a gatehouse in the form of an overhanging battlement to protect the entrance of a castle.

Baroque. Period roughly from 1600 to 1700; also applied to painting, sculpture, music, literature, and the life style of the period.

Barrel Vault. Half-cylindrical vault, usually over an oblong space.

Base. Lowest form of a structure. In a column, the part upon which the shaft rests.

Basilica. Name derived from the Roman assembly hall. In medieval architecture, a church with its nave higher than its aisles and an apse at one end.

Bastion. Projection from the outer wall of a castle or fort.

Battlement. Indented parapet. Openings are called embrasures or crenelles (crenellated) and raised parts are called merlons.

Belfry. Part of a tower or turret in which bells are hung.

Belvedere. A pavilion, turret, or lantern on a house. Also a standing or a lookout tower. *See also,* Gazebo.

Bull's-Eye Window. Round or oval window with glazing bars radiating from a circular center.

Buttress. Gothic method of support by means of

masonry or brickwork which is built against a wall to give it stability or to counter the thrusts of an arch or vault.

Byzantine. Early Christian architecture characterized by Roman and Oriental elements.

Campanile. Italian word for a free-standing bell tower.

Carolean. English period embracing reigns of Charles I (1625–49) and Charles II (1660–85).

Cartouche. Shaped tablet enclosed in an ornamental frame or scroll, usually bearing inscription or heraldic device.

Caryatid. Sculptured female figure used as a column.

Castle. Fortified building; a place for defense; a stronghold.

Cathedral. A bishop's church, named for the *cathedra,* or throne.

Cenotaph. Greek word for empty grave; a memorial to the dead.

Chapel. Prayer room in a castle or dwelling house; now used to describe a small church.

Chevron. Zigzag molding characteristic of Norman architecture.

Chinoiserie. Style incorporating Chinese elements, especially characteristic of the eighteenth-century rococo period.

Classicism. Style or tendency originally derived from ancient Greece or Rome.

Cloister. Covered walk around the courtyard of a monastery.

Colonial Style. Style which was developed in the eastern United States and Canada by European colonists using classical and Renaissance elements.

Colonnade. A columned walk without arches; frequently a feature of baroque and neoclassical architecture.

Column. Vertical supporting member; in classical architecture it consists of a base, shaft, and capital.

Composite Capital. The most elaborate of five orders, having many variations. It combines the volutes, or spiral scrolls, of the Ionic with the foliate bell of the Corinthian.

Constructivism. A Russian movement which had considerable influence on architecture and decoration throughout the 1920's. Abstract forms of concrete were juxtaposed to large windows of plate glass.

Corinthian. Bell-shaped capital ornamented with acanthus, olive, or laurel leaves from which eight small, spiral scrolls emerge. The shaft is usually fluted.

Court. Open area, usually enclosed by a wall, in front or behind a building.

Crenellated. *See* Battlement.

Crypt. Subterranean burial place in churches.

Cupola. A small, domed vaulted roof or small domed turret built upon a roof.

Cutwater. Wedge-shaped end of the pier of a bridge which breaks the current of water.

Decorated Style. Period of English Gothic roughly from 1270 to 1350; characterized by decorative forms.

Diamond Ashlar. Flat, pyramid-shaped, dressed wall-stone, found especially in neoclassical architecture of eighteenth century.

Donjon. French for the castle keep, or dungeon.

Dormer. Roof window.

Doric Capital. Capital distinguished by the rectangular blocks (triglyphs) between the plain or decorated spaces (metopes) in its frieze. Greek Doric has no base and a fluted shaft, while Roman has a base plus a fluted or unfluted shaft.

Drawbridge. Bridge over a moat or ditch surrounding a castle or fortified town.

Early English. Period of earliest English Gothic, roughly 1175 to 1270; between Norman and Decorated styles.

Egyptian Revival. Adoption of Egyptian forms and details as a result of archaeological discoveries around 1800.

Elevation. External front of any building; also a drawing which shows any one side of a building.

Elizabethan. English architecture of the reign of Queen Elizabeth I (1558–1603); characterized by free use of Renaissance design and ornament but incorporating late Gothic elements, too.

Empire. French classicism of Napoleonic empire (1800–30); characterized by use of Greek and Egyptian motifs.

Epitaph. Memorial tablet for the dead.

Façade. Face or front of a building, especially the principal front.

Fanlight. Originally a semicircular or fan-shaped window above a Georgian door. Now used to describe any window above a door.

Festoon. Carved, modeled, or painted garland or an array of flowers, fruits, or leaves suspended between two points.

Fluting. The vertical grooving on the shaft of a column.

Folly. A sometimes fantastic structure usually set in a park or garden.

Fortress. *See* Castle.

Forum. Roman term for the central square of a city.

Fosse. Ditch or moat.

Frieze. Decorative band, usually horizontal, along a wall or entablature. May be painted, carved, ornamented, or figured.

Gable. The triangular portion of wall at the end of a roof. Main types are: *Dutch gable*—curved or shaped and topped by pediment; *crow-step*—with stepped sides; *hipped gable*—the uppermost part slopes back; and *shaped gable*—one with multi-curved sides.

Gargoyle. A waterspout in the form of a carved, grotesque human or animal head, usually projecting from the top of a wall.

Gothic. Great epoch of European art and architecture from the mid-twelfth century to the end of the Middle Ages; in some countries extending into the sixteenth century. Also used to indicate a strange and bizarre variation of the style.

Gothic Revival. An attempt to recreate decorative forms of Gothic. Began in eighteenth-century England; also encouraged by John Ruskin in the nineteenth century.

Greek Cross. Cross with four arms of equal length.

Grotesque. Form of decoration composed of fanciful animal and human forms.

Half-Timbering. Form of a building in which the main structure—the walls and partitions—are built as timber framework and filled with plaster, brick, stone, wattle and daub, etc. Used from the fifteenth to the eighteenth centuries.

Historicism. Stylistic tendency, especially in the second half of nineteenth century, to make use of features from past epochs.

Ionic Order. Antique style originating in the Ionian Islands; characterized by voluted capitals and canalized column shafts.

Jugendstil. Style named after the famous Munich periodical launched in 1896. *See* Art Nouveau.

Keep. Great, main tower of a castle.

Lantern. The very top of a dome; usually cylindrical or polygonal, with windows, and crowned by a small dome.

Lintel. Horizontal cross member spanning an opening or door.

Loophole. *See* Arrow Loophole.

Louis Seize. Period of transition to classicism in France under Louis XVI (1774–92). Similar to rococo but more restrained.

Lunette. Semicircular space above doors or windows.

Mansard Roof. *See* Roof.

Mausoleum. Building designed to house tombs.

Medallion. Round or oval decoration usually of stucco, sometimes with an effigy or profile, used to fill a blank space.

Minaret. Tower close to a mosque, usually pointed, from which the call to prayer is made.

Moat. Deep, wide ditch surrounding a castle, house, or town and usually filled with water.

Monastery. The complete complex for the monastic life: living quarters, church, farm buildings, garden, library, and school.

Mosaic. A technique for the decoration of walls, floors, etc., consisting of small cubes of colored stone or glass pressed into a soft, damp base of mortar or cement.

Mosque. Islamic church or place of worship.

Mullion. Straight tracery of Gothic windows.

Neoclassical. A style which dominated Europe between 1760 and 1790 and was the product of a new interest in antiquity which resulted from archaeological discoveries made in Rome and in the newly-excavated cities of Herculaneum and Pompeii, and others in Asia Minor and Greece. The logic, taste, and imagination of the ancients helped create a new classical style. In England, the leading exponents were Robert Adam, James "Athenian" Stuart, and Sir William Chambers. In the United Staates the leader was Benjamin Latrobe (1766–1820), the architect of the Hall of Representatives, Washington, and the Bank of Philadelphia.

Neo-Gothic. A nineteenth-century trend which aimed at reviving Gothic forms of architecture and applied design.

Niche. Recess in a wall, usually semicircular and arched, where a statue or other object may be placed.

Norman. Period of early English architecture during the eleventh and twelfth centuries before Gothic and following Saxon.

Obelisk. An Egyptian cult symbol for the sun-god. A tall, tapering stone pillar having four sides and a pyramidal top. Used in small sizes as a decoration on façades of baroque and neoclassical buildings. Today a form of memorial.

Onion-Roof. Tower top or hood of Oriental origin, shaped like onion, frequently found in Russian architecture, also South German baroque.

Orangery. Gallery or building in which orange trees and other plants are grown. Usually a feature of palaces and country houses of the seventeenth and eighteenth centuries.

Order. The essential components of a complete order are a column base, a shaft and a capital, and an entablature with architrave, frieze, and cornice. Size and proportion vary with each order. The three Greek orders are Doric, Ionic, and Corinthian. The Romans added two more: Tuscan and Composite. *See also* entries under these headings.

Pagoda. Temple or sacred building in India, China, and Southeastern Asia. Usually of pyramidal form built over relics of a Buddhist saint.

Palladian. Style named after Andrea Palladio (1508–80), who exerted great influence through his *Four Books of Architecture* (1570). Characterized by severely dignified and monumental adoption of Roman style.

Parapet. Low wall at the edge of a bridge, gallery, balcony, or above the cornice of a building.

Patio. Inner courtyard of a Spanish house.

Pavilion. Originally a term for a square tent. A detached pleasure house in a park or garden, or a small annex to a larger building.

Pedestal. Support for a column, statue, urn, etc.

Pediment. Lower projecting part of a wall, pillar, or column.

Piazza. Open public place surrounded by buildings.

Pinnacle. Slender decorative tower, usually found on Gothic buttresses and on the corners of towers and gables.

Plinth. Base of a column, a pillar, or a statue.

Portal. Any kind of imposing entrance.

Portcullis. Heavy iron or wooden grating built to slide vertically in grooves cut at the sides of an entrance gateway to a medieval castle.

Quadrangle. Inner square, rectangular space, or courtyard. *See also* Court.

Quattrocento. In Italy, the usual term for the fifteenth century, the period of the early Renaissance.

Queen Anne Style. English period of Queen Anne's reign (1702–14) which includes the greatest achievements of Wren and the rise of English baroque (Vanbrugh and Hawksmoor). Term also applies to elegant domestic style principally executed in red brick; also characterized by sash windows and hipped roofs.

Quoins. Corner stones at the angle of a building.

Rampart. Protective stone wall surrounding a castle or fort.

Refectory. Dining hall of a monastery or college.

Regency. English style characterized by chaste elegant detail, typified in the terraces of Brighton, Cheltenham, and Tunbridge Wells.

Rococo. Style of the late baroque period characterized by the transformation of classical ornament into elegant and sometimes fanciful forms seen in plasterwork, chimney pieces, staircases, and furniture.

Romanesque. Comprehensive term for a style of early Christian architecture deriving from the Roman roughly during the period 1000–1300. Characterized by round arches, thick walls, heavy columns, and capitals.

Roof. Cover over the walls of a building. Main types include: *lean-to*—a roof with a single slope; *gable-roof*—simple triangular-shaped roof formed by pairs of rafters; *tent-roof*—triangular-shaped but sides are sloped inwards to apex in center; *hipped roof*—ends are sloped inwards instead of being gabled; *half-hipped*—ends partly gabled and partly sloped; *Mansard*—a roof with two degrees of slopes, where the lower is more acute than the upper.

Rotunda. Round building, or the round part of a building, or the circular space under a dome.

Russian Style. Style of church architecture developed in Russia from the Byzantine. Baroque forms are characteristic, as well as onion-shaped caps or hoods to towers which are often richly guilded.

Spire. Tall, tapering structure in the form of an elongated pyramid or polygonal cone erected on top of a tower, turret, roof, etc.

Stucco. A technique of adornment of Oriental origin, but used in Europe in the early Middle Ages, using a mixture of plaster and water with lime and sand. Requires great skill because corrections cannot be made once the material has set. Method is suitable for representation of human figures and ornamentation.

Terrace. A level promenade, usually in front of a building; also applicable to rows of houses built in uniform style.

Tudor. English period (1485–1603) extending from the late Gothic style of perpendicular to the end of Queen Elizabeth I's reign. Half-timbering and brick are characteristic materials.

Turret. Small decorative tower usually set on the ridge of a gable roof.

Vault. Arched roof, or ceiling, built in masonry or cast. Usually massive, strengthened by ribs.

Weather Boarding. Overlapping horizontal boards fixed on the external walls of timber-framed buildings. Common in Southeastern and Southern England, also in the United States where it is known as *clapboard*.

Index

Edited by Diane Casella Hines
Designed by James Craig and Robert Fillie
Set in 10 point Optima by Brown Bros. Linotypers, Inc.
Printed and bound in Japan by Toppan Printing Company, Ltd.